Christian Faith
for the
Empirically Minded

CHARLES E GARRISON

WESTBOW
P R E S S®
A DIVISION OF THOMAS NELSON
& ZONDERVAN

Scriptures taken from the Holy Bible, New International Version®, NIV®. Copyright © 1973, 1978, 1984, 2011 by Biblica, Inc.™ Used by permission of Zondervan. All rights reserved worldwide. www.zondervan.com The "NIV" and "New International Version" are trademarks registered in the United States Patent and Trademark Office by Biblica, Inc.™

WestBow Press books may be ordered through booksellers or by contacting:

WestBow Press
A Division of Thomas Nelson & Zondervan
1663 Liberty Drive
Bloomington, IN 47403
www.westbowpress.com
1 (866) 928-1240

Because of the dynamic nature of the Internet, any web addresses or links contained in this book may have changed since publication and may no longer be valid. The views expressed in this work are solely those of the author and do not necessarily reflect the views of the publisher, and the publisher hereby disclaims any responsibility for them.

Any people depicted in stock imagery provided by Thinkstock are models, and such images are being used for illustrative purposes only. Certain stock imagery © Thinkstock.

ISBN: 978-1-5127-8051-2 (sc)
ISBN: 978-1-5127-8052-9 (hc)
ISBN: 978-1-5127-8050-5 (e)

Library of Congress Control Number: 2017904412

Print information available on the last page.

WestBow Press rev. date: 4/24/2017

Contents

Contents

Prologue

I am both a Christian and an empiricist. Being an empiricist means that I am convinced that empirical knowledge is the most reliable knowledge available and thus I believe in science and the scientific method. To know something empirically is to know it first hand through the senses. It is direct experience. "Seeing is believing," goes the truism. It is possible, of course, to be mistaken as to what we think we have seen. Witnesses to a crime often contradict each other. Illusionists as magicians entertain us by making us think we have seen something that we know is impossible. We are, however, most likely to be legitimately certain about that which is experienced empirically.

But, I am also a Christian and it is sometimes claimed that this means I am to believe in Christ even though there is no empirical evidence. Indeed, the Apostle Paul seemed to separate faith from what is empirical when he wrote that "[Christians] live by faith and not by sight." (2 Cor. 5:7) The third century Christian theologian, Tertulian, famously said, "I believe because it is absurd." To believe without evidence does not appeal to me. So I ask: Is there empirical support for Christianity? Must my Christian faith be without support by the empiricism that I believe is the most reliable source of knowledge?

It is quite the opposite! The New Testament regarded empirical knowledge as valuable. In introducing the biblical book of Luke, the author wrote, "I myself have carefully investigated everything from the beginning." (Luke 1:3) In Peter's sermon on the Day of Pentecost he declared, "We are all witnesses of [the resurrection]." (Acts 2:32)

John began his first letter with the declaration that they had "heard . . . seen . . . touched" the "Word of Life" through Jesus. (1 John 1:1) Another biblical author, Peter, wrote, "We did not follow cleverly devised stories . . . we were eyewitnesses. (2 Peter 1:16) Indeed, Christians were told to be prepared and willing to "give the reason for the hope that you have." (1 Peter 3:15) These statements give priority to empirical experience.

Jesus also recognized the value of empirical evidence. When Thomas touched Jesus' body and realized that it was Jesus himself, Jesus told him, "Because you have seen me, you have believed. Blessed are those who have not seen yet have believed." (John 20:29) Such empirical experience was available only to a relatively few people who were contemporaries to that place and time. Today, we are all "those who have not seen." Does this mean that the Christian should try to believe even if there is no empirical support?

It is clear that having empirical evidence—to have seen as Thomas did—is not available to us today. We cannot know if Mary was a virgin, that Jesus walked on water, or that people who were dead were brought back to life. We have never seen any of these so how can we believe? Millions do believe, of course, but many do not and many would like to believe but find it difficult.

We cannot know if these things happened and it is fruitless to try or even to be bothered by the fact that we cannot know. We simply can't. This does not mean that there are no empirical bases that can be explored that might give us insight in the search for truth. What I want to do is search for empirical groundings derived from science or other empirical sources that contribute to a reasonable evaluation of the reliability of the Christian faith. People may "walk by faith and not by sight" but they can still seek to discover what "sights" exist. Thus, we explore: What are the facts? What is empirically grounded? What can I know and how certain should I be?

For many Christians, the perceived lack of empirical support for their faith is not a problem. They have been taught the faith, they believe that it works, and this validates it for them. They have no significant doubts. The claim that empirical grounding is important does not resonate with them. For me, the presence or absence of empirical grounding is important and I am not alone in this.

For an empiricist, the question of evidence that supports a claimed fact is always important. That something works does not make it true. Medical research has long been aware of the placebo effect. This is that if one believes that medicine has been ingested there may be recovery even though it was a placebo and had no medicinal content. This is the "faith factor" that is characteristic of humans. Believing in something can have consequences even if there is no basis for what is believed. Herbert Benson long advocated that humans should consider the "placebo effect" as a positive fact and marshal the power of faith as a benefit.[1] It is valuable if belief in a pill brings healing even if it has no medicinal value. From this perspective, to have faith in a Christianity that produced the fruits of love, justice, and security would be good even if Christianity did not have any factual basis.

History, however, is strewn with examples where belief in a religion produced injustice, harm, and unnecessary suffering. An often-cited example is the pyramid at Cholula in central Mexico. Human sacrifice there was regularly carried out because they believed that if the gods were not "fed regularly with human blood, the universe would fall apart." Religion required it. This was, as Peter Berger noted, but one of many "pyramids of sacrifice" over which religions have presided.[2] That a faith works does

---

[1] Herbert Benson, *Beyond the Relaxation Response* (New York: Berkley Books, 1984).
[2] Peter Berger, *Pyramids of Sacrifice* (Garden City: Anchor Books, 1976), 1—6.

not necessarily mean that it is true or good. Although a grounded faith can also go astray, the inductive grounded method provides one important perspective with which to review religion. To be skeptical of religious claims has much to commend itself. Jesus was skeptical of much of the religious practice he encountered. An unsupported religious faith can be good but it can also be very harmful.

The empirically minded always want to search further: What is the evidence? I really want to know if there is empirical support for Christianity. If there is none, so be it. But, if there is evidence whether strong or weak, I want to know. I want a grounded faith and not a placebo faith. The pages that follow are lines of thinking that make sense and have helped me to clarify my Christian faith. I am sure there are other additional factors that could be included. My hope for the reader is that it will clarify your faith also.

In a short book such as this, I do not explore in any detail but I do point out some pathways and some authors I have found helpful. In our contemporary world, there are empirical conclusions that are considered to be barriers to the Christian faith but may not be found to be such. There are also supportive empirical findings.

Chapter

1

What Can We Know for Sure?

*A*lthough I firmly believe that empirical knowledge is the most certain method for knowing, it does not provide an easy path to certitude. The King of Siam declared in the musical *The King and I* that there were times he was not sure of what he absolutely knew. "Very often," he explained, "I find confusion in conclusion I concluded long ago." When we carefully examine the factual evidence on which we base our beliefs—especially in important matters—we, like the king, will conclude we cannot be sure about many of the things we know. This first chapter is extended and perhaps laborious for a brief book but it sets out a fundamental approach to the matter of what we can know for sure.

When we think seriously about what we can know

with certainty, agnosticism can become a very attractive option. How can we ever have certainty about an invisible God? To decide to be an agnostic then may become appealing. The problem with the agnostic conclusion is that we still must live our lives and to live is to inescapably base our lives on ideas. The king, like all of us, must decide even if he is not certain. Even that about which we are certain may turn out to be wrong.

There is a maxim that says, "Whether we philosophize or not, we must philosophize." That is, each of us has a collection of ideas that form a foundation upon which we live our lives. We may not be aware of what these ideas are. We may not be able to recall where we got them or how valid they may be. Whether examined or not, we act on the ideas embedded in our minds. We make decisions based upon what we assume to be a good life, what it means to be human, what I should expect from others, and what others should expect of me. All of the most significant decisions we make in life such as marriage, career, and health care are ultimately matters for which we cannot be certain. But we must decide anyway. To refuse to make decisions because we cannot be certain is guaranteed to be harmful.

Even though we are uncertain, it is reasonable to ask if one set of ideas is likely to be better than another. We need to acknowledge our ignorance but we do not need to be paralyzed by it. We can examine ideas about which we are uncertain to see what is the best fit with what is known. To act as if we have no philosophy is to act without awareness of the ideas that are driving our decisions. It is to choose a direction without knowing why. It is to act based on assumptions without examining the validity of those assumptions.

Everyday Empiricism and Scientific Empiricism

We all believe in and practice "everyday empiricism." That is, we have the most confidence about what is true in that which we directly experience. We also consider as true much that we may not have experienced but have learned from others in the culture and the sub-cultures in which we have lived. One definition of culture is that it is shared responses made by people to the opportunities and depravations they encounter. As we interact with others we share with them and learn from them what seems most likely to be true or false. Culture instructs us as to what has been thought to be true. When the culturally defined truth is congruent with our own experiences, our confidence in it increases. When culture and experience are not congruent, we may try to understand the inconsistency. We also may come to doubt and ultimately reject the culturally prescribed truth.

To illustrate this point with an absurdly simple example, if I see a tree I will walk around it rather than try to walk through it. I have solid empirical experience with trees. The experience of other people with trees—they walk around them, lean on them, or climb them—confirms my experience. What one believes about marriage and other important matters is so much more complex but is still directly related to the experiences we have had and what we have accepted from our culture.

The Pew Research Center reported in 2009 that one in five Americans have experienced ghosts and one in seven have consulted a psychic.[3] I find this very difficult to believe although I do have confidence in Pew research.

---

[3] For discussion, see T. M. Luhrmann, "Conjuring Up Our Own Gods," *New York Times*, October 13, 2013.

I have lived in a culture and subculture where belief in ghosts has not been expressed. If anyone I know has seen a ghost that experience has not been shared to me. If I were to see a ghost I think that I would not believe it. There have been places and times past in which most people have believed in ghosts. Surveys such as the one by Pew indicate that there are still such places in our society where ghosts are considered to be real. Such is the way with culture. It defines reality and is convincing. It also can be questioned and altered when it does not make sense of everyday experience.

Everyday empiricism is empirical because it is based on experience—our own and what we derive from interaction with others. It is "everyday" because it is how we live in everyday life. Culture does not happen willy-nilly. The self does not form willy-nilly. Culture and self are products of specific social processes. That is, they are specific to the individual and the individual's social context.

Everyday empiricism is empirical but it is not scientific. To be scientific, empiricism must be systematic, controlled, measurable, and replicable. We should not need to be reminded that the scientific methodology has been inordinately productive. Yet, in our normal use of its products this is easy to forget. As I sit in an air-conditioned room and speak to a family member who is hundreds of miles away, I do not think about science but it is the application of science that has made what was in the past impossible to now become everyday routine.

Neither the comforts nor conveniences we experience in our devices—such as the air conditioning and cell phones—would be possible without the fundamental methodology of scientific research. The cell phone did not just happen by discovery. It was developed from a scientific empiricism that explored and learned about invisible process and utilized a world that was and is unseen. We would not know that it existed in our every day empiricism. Science discovered it and our devices are reminders. Empirical science can make mistakes but it remains the most reliable way of knowing.[4]

We live our lives between what we know through

---

[4] For a discussion of the errors made by prominent scientists, see Mario Livio, *Brilliant Blunders: from Darwin to Einstein—Colossal Mistakes by Great Scientists that Changed Our Understanding of Life and the Universe* (New York: Simon and Schuster, 2014).

the empiricism of everyday life and the empiricism that science reports. Some people believe in their own experiences but distrust science. Others trust science but may distrust some of their own experiences. One person may know little about evolution but believes it because it is presented as scientific. Another person finds evolution to be too far from life experience and considers it speculative and unpersuasive. Most of us have neither absolute confidence in our life experiences nor absolute confidence in reported scientific findings. We probably live somewhere on a spectrum between these poles.

Science is an extremely valuable aid in stimulating our awareness of diverse realities. Scientific explorations from the quantum world of quarks to the multiple universes and all intermediate points—even such as the intricate biological system that keeps the eyes appropriately moist—are examples of the innumerable ways science has expanded our awareness of the awesomeness of the universe.

Science opens to us the awareness that the world is not what it seems to be in everyday life. Everyday empiricism can mislead us. Science takes us beyond the everyday empiricism to explore what may, in fact, prove to be the opposite of our everyday experiences. It is important to be aware of this reality.

From physics we learn that solid objects are not solid at all. Empty space is not empty. This is a very different world from what we think it is. The gadgets of our everyday world—such as the already mentioned cellphones can be reminders of this unseen reality if we will only notice. The invisible communication link in every cell phone and all of our remote devices can be reminders that the world we see is only part of the world. I click my remote and the car door locks. This invisible signal may have passed through an internal wall, an external wall, and the exterior of the car. I was in Spain and clicked the cell phone number for my daughter in Chicago and she answered even though she was climbing a hill in Mexico. All of this is very ordinary in our experience today but it is an applied technology of processes found in an invisible reality we could never know through everyday experience. That we cannot see and have no reason to believe that they could exist does not mean that they are not real. If we will but notice, this access to an invisible reality is an important reminder. They work because physicists have explored this invisible world and applied their findings for our everyday use. Before we had such gadgets as cell phones and remote control devices we could not imagine that these invisible factors existed.

Our eyes see and our ears hear only that reality that falls within the bandwidths of human eyes and ears. If our eyes or ears had different components, we would see and hear a very different world. Physics tells us that there is more to the universe than what we can observe in everyday life and that it is very different from what we do observe.

Carlo Rovelli has written about examples of this invisible world, "If a person who has lived at sea level meets up with his twin who has lived in the mountains, he will find that his sibling is slightly older than he."[5] He adds: "Physics describes a colorful and amazing world where universes explode, space collapses into bottomless holes, time sags and slows near a planet."[6] Furthermore,

_____

[5] Carlo Rovelli, *Seven Brief Lessons on Physics* (New York: Riverhead Books, 2016) 10.
[6] Ibid., 11.

"The clues point toward something profoundly different from our experience of matter, space, and time."[7] John Polkinghorne, an eminent physicist, has written that, "Our ability to understand the subatomic quantum world [is] totally different from the macroscopic world of everyday happenings. [It requires] counterintuitive ways of thinking for its understanding."[8] This means that the "real world" of physics is not the "real world" as I experience it. I do not doubt the world that physics tells me exists but it is not what I experience. Physics compels me to acknowledge the alternative realities between what science tells me and what I experience.

I accept what physics tells me about the quantum world but have found that I still do not think that way. My basic way of thinking is that of the "clockwork" view where natural law is inviolate and cause and effect can potentially explain everything when the technology is developed to observe and measure. I asked a physicist why I am unable to let go of the Newtonian approach. He quickly responded that this was true simply because

---

[7] Ibid., 49.

[8] *Science and Religion in Quest of Truth* (New Haven: Yale University Press, 2011), 71.

my everyday experience is in the observable Newtonian reality and not the unseen quantum world of physics.

So I try to remind myself regularly that this world I learn about in physics is real even though I do not experience it. The useful products resulting from the world of physics has given us innumerable applications and I use them daily without thought. Thus, I do not see how my wireless devices work but they do and I remind myself that they work because of this invisible reality discovered in physics. So it is important to repeat, the "real world" is not at all like the world of everyday empirical experience. Today we have good scientific evidence of the existence of these invisible realities. Should these not compel us to be open-minded to the possibility of other realities unknown in everyday empiricism? I must remember the fact that there can be realities unrecognized in everyday experience. Christianity asks us to believe in such a reality unseen to everyday empiricism and the example of quantum physics should forewarn us not to consider it to be impossible. This is not evidence for the Christian view of the world but it is an excellent reason to keep the mind open for evidence.

Empiricism's Adjustments

The methodology of science requires observation and replication but there are many areas where this is not possible and science adjusts its method as needed. For examples, neither the origin of the universe nor biological evolution can be directly observed and neither one can be replicated. The sub-atomic world of matter has not so far been amenable to direct observation. The values of science are observed in such research but the research project must be adjusted to correspond to the nature of the available data. This is not a compromise of methodology but an adjustment to the realities of the subject matter.

So to do research in quantum physics requires that it adjust to the nature of its data. In doing so, it has found that it cannot predict the specific effect of a specific cause. It has found, instead, that it can predict the probability that a cause will have an effect. In this, Polkinghorne observes, physics has become statistical—its predictions are probabilistic.[9] It is not a mechanized clockwork of cause and effect as in Newtonian physics.

---

[9] Ibid., 36.

Polkinghorne has emphasized that in moving from the language of "certain proof," science has replaced it with the search for the "best explanation."[10] For this, he uses the term *verisimilitude*. When science cannot use the experimental method with replication and direct observation, it can assemble what data is known and then look for what theory fits best with these facts. With verisimilitude, the findings will be probabilistic. This is a necessary methodological adjustment that occurs in many areas of science. Cosmology, for example, cannot study the origins of the universe as such but it can take what data it has and ask what is the best theoretical fit— that is to say, what is verisimilitudenous.

Social science holds to the values of science but it also has recognized in its methodology and analysis of data that it produces probabilistic conclusions that use a verisimilitudinous theoretical understanding. Historical events cannot be replicated. Psychological and social processes are expressed by word and behavior but they are never strictly facts. They require interpretation. For

---

[10] Ibid., 71.

some, this seems to establish that social science is not really a science. Even so, the social sciences can adhere to the values of empiricism and adjust the methods of research accordingly. This is the best that can be done whether the subject at hand is cosmology, archaeology, or history. Such probabilistic research has been extremely valuable whether it is seen as a science of not.

Polkinghorne contends that the verisimilitudinous approach science uses is also applicable to the study of Christianity. [11] He advocates an approach to the study of religion in which we assemble all relevant information that is known and then ask what theory is the "best fit." We cannot prove that there is a God because we do not have direct access to the data. What we can do is gather all of the facts that we can know and then hypothesize from these empirical bases what best fits with all that we do know. Polkinghorne is a physicist who has studied much and written much about the application

---

[11] John Polkinghorne has written about this in many books. Examples are *Beyond Science: The Wider Human Context*, Cambridge: Cambridge University Press, 1996; Also, *One World: The Interaction of Science and Theology*, Princeton: Princeton University Press, 1986.

of the verisimilitudinous approach to determine what hypotheses about Christianity best fits with all of the reality that is known.

Natural science, social science, and religion are all different phenomena but they exist in the same world. Empiricism as our most reliable way of understanding can be applied in varying ways adjusting its methods for the nature of the data. Findings that are in the probabilistic and the verisimilitudinous approach are widely used in science and so, Polkinghorne argues, they are similarly applicable in the study of religion.

To summarize, Christianity as well as physics calls for us to believe there is a world very different from the everyday world of experience. Physics requires us to be able to think in a way that is counter-intuitive to the world we observe. Should we not be open to the possibility that there are other aspects of the universe where reality may call for counter-intuitive thinking as well? Christianity has not produced gadgets to validate itself but there is still significant evidence of an unseen spiritual world as well. If there is such, this is an important application to how we live. It may be true or it may be false but it is not trivial. In this purview, it is likely to be erroneous to close the mind and cling too much to a Newtonian view.

What we do know is that religion exists—it is a component of human experience. We have data. What does it mean? It is like many areas of human behavior that are similarly experiential and not given to direct empirical study. Studies of marriage are an example. Marriage exists and experiences of it can be compared through the lens of various disciplines like psychology, sociology and history. The findings will be probabilistic. They will not meet the criteria for the laboratory experiment. They are, however, experiential data and vitally important. They do seek to follow the scientific methodology necessarily adjusted to the nature of the data. This is the claim Polkinghorne has made for the study of Christianity.

Distinctions in Religious Phenomena

Religion has some characteristics that require specific adjustments in the use of empiricism. Religion is very much concerned with the meaning of events whereas science is unable to deal with meaning. Lightning in everyday empiricism seems capricious yet when Martin Luther was struck by lightning, he believed it was literally God speaking to him and his response was a vow to become a monk. Scientific laws of physics, however, can explain why lightning strikes where and when it does and that it follows natural law and is predictable if the precise conditions are known. Thus lightning in our culture is believed to be a phenomenon of natural law that is neither capricious nor a message from God.

Science, however, cannot discover meaning. To Luther, the lightning strike was meaningful. It was a message from God. To those of us who accept science's explanation of lightning as a natural process, it does not have meaning. We seek safe shelter during a lightning storm but it is because we accept the scientific explanation although we have no method to determine specifically where it will strike. If, in fact, there was a God who was sending Luther a message, science would be unable to discover it.

Polkinghorne explains the distinction between the explanation of science and meaning in the making of tea. "The kettle is boiling both because gas heats the water (the scientific explanation) and because I want to make a cup of tea (an explanation invoking purpose)."[12] Why Polkinghorne is fixing tea may be because he is British, because he wants to relax, or because he is going to be host to a visitor. These answers involve cause and effect in terms of purpose—that is to say human meaning.

Polkinghorne has observed that "a scientist, speaking as a scientist, can say no more about music than that it is vibrations in the air, but speaking as a person there would surely be much more to say about the mysterious way in which a temporal succession of sounds can give us access to a timeless realm of beauty."[13] There may or may not be meaning in lightning but humans do find important meaning in many phenomena including music.

Meaning is an empirically verified human experience even if science cannot deal with it. As humans, we seek what is meaningful and when experience seems meaningless, it is harmful. Indeed, meaning is not only a mental feeling but it can have a powerful effect on the biological organism. The placebo effect, already mentioned, is necessary as a control in testing medical developments and this demonstrates the effect of the

---

[12] *Science and Religion in Quest of Truth*, 21.
[13] Ibid., 4.

mind on the biological processes of the individual. Faith has medical consequences.

Another example of human meaning and its impact on the biological organism can be demonstrated by the effect of touch. If someone touches you and you welcome the touch it is a totally different physiological experience than when someone touches you against your wish. The biological stimulation may be exactly the same but the experience will be totally different. The meaning that the individual attaches to the touching alters the biological phenomenon.

Meaning is not ephemeral but fundamental to human experience. Humans insist on the search for meaning. The survivor of a mass shooting asks why it happened and often is reported to have asked why he or she survived. There is an assumption that there must be a meaning. Viktor Frankl's book, *Man's Search for Meaning,* made the case very well that the human animal is always involved in the search for meaning and the consequences of the search are crucial for the life story.

A second distinction in the study of religion is that Christianity places importance on certain unique events that are claimed to have happened. Science cannot consider unique phenomena. When Luther was struck by lightning, he considered it a unique experience—a message to him from God—and not inherent in all lightning. That there are natural laws that explain the location of a lightning strike does not mean that it was meaningless in Luther's case. As Polkinghorne reminds us, "Science is concerned with what usually happens."[14] It requires replication—that is, an "unproblematic repetition of the same phenomena."[15] Unique events can occur but they cannot be evaluated scientifically. He continues, "All [science] can say about the resurrection [of Jesus] is that usually dead people stay dead, a fact as clearly known in the first century as it is today."[16] To claim that a dead person returned to life should be met with extreme skepticism and alternative explanations carefully considered. The empirically oriented will look for alternative explanations that could be more probable. Beyond this, such an event cannot be subjected to scientific examination.

---

[14] Ibid., 96.
[15] Ibid.,3.
[16] Ibid., 96.

Recently I decided to travel to South America. This decision could not be explained scientifically because it could not be replicated. To decide to make a second trip would be a different decision and not a replication. For someone else to decide to make a trip to South America would be a different decision and not a replication. My wife, however, was not at all surprised by my travel decision and can explain it with several cause and effect factors which demonstrate that the decision was not capricious or random but highly probable. Everyday empiricism can sometimes go where scientific empiricism cannot in terms of both meaning and predictiion.

As important as empiricism has proven to be, it does not rule out the value of non-empirical insights. The Buddha meditated for five years after which he had gained insights that have benefited people for centuries. This is not uncommon. Mohammad spent a long time in a cave. Jesus spent forty days in the wilderness. Advocates of transcendental meditation cite numerous research findings to support the values people report from the practice of meditation. The insight may not be empirically provable but the consequences can be empirically examined.

It is common in creative thinking and in the arts for it to be expressed that there is an invisible and unconscious process that has taken place. The composer may report that the music just came to the person who wrote it down. People can on occasion read what they have written and discover dimensions in it of which they were unaware. What people respond to or do not respond to can also be puzzling. Why is there a play that moves audiences written by an author whose other plays do not work? Why are some artists unappreciated in their lifetimes but later discovered and believed to have been creative geniuses? As uncertain as we can be about such descriptions, the sense that creativity can be revelatory is another realm of human experience to be pondered. Mahatma Gandhi identified as one of the seven deadly sins, "Science without humanity." Blaise Pascal wrote that "the heart has reasons that "the head cannot know." The arts and humanities are important ways of knowing to be nurtured as well as the valued empiricism.

What can we know for sure? In spite of the various ways we can have knowledge there is very little of that which is most important that we can know with certainty. We do, however, have resources that can be utilized rather than simply being agnostic. We have everyday empiricism. We have the empiricism of the sciences. We have the devices—remote controls, laptops, the cloud—to remind us that there are unseen realities that everyday empiricism would have never imagined.

We also have insights from arts and humanities. We can explore for the probabilities—what might be true. We can think, reflect, and correct our decisions based upon our experiences and those of others. We can utilize empiricism and its methodology according to the best data available. We can accept that our conclusions will be probabilistic and versimilitudinous but they are far more helpful than ignorance. We can weigh and balance the various insights.

Polkinghorne has urged us to use these same standards in the study of religion that we apply to other topics of study. We do not have the empirical data to prove there is an invisible God but we do have data and we can submit it to a verisimilistic analysis. We can ask what theories fit best with what we know. We can explore for empirical evidence.

Chapter

2

A Starting Point

*T*he empirical search must have a starting point that cannot be doubted and there is a traditional one that is persuasive. It is what Descartes wrote in the seventeenth century, "I think, therefore I am." Philosophers have expressed it in the question, "Why is there something instead of nothing?"[17] The question may sound silly but as Stephen Hawking noted, "Ever since the dawn of civilization, people have craved an understanding of the underlying order of the world, why it is as it is and why it exists at all."[18] The philosopher Wittgenstein observed,

---

[17] Heidegger is often credited with elevating this question in metaphysics though it was earlier stated by Gottfried Leibniz in 1697.

[18] Quoted by John Bowker, *God: A Very Short Introduction* (Oxford: Oxford University Press, 2014), 26.

"Not *how* the world is, but *that* it is, is the mystery."[19] The question inherently accepts that there is something and this can be for our consideration an undoubtable foundation. "To the question, 'How do I know I exist?' a professor famously replied, 'And who's asking?'"[20] We cannot doubt that the world exists and we are in it.

In reflecting on the existence of the universe itself, a natural progression is to realize that this fact is truly awesome. Abraham Heschel has discussed the importance of cultivating our awareness of this awesomeness. His statement warrants a careful reading:

> In Biblical language the religious man is not called 'believer,' as he is for example in Islam (mu'min), but yare *hashem* (awe of God). There is thus only one way to wisdom: awe. Forfeit your sense of awe, let your conceit diminish your ability to revere, and the universe becomes a market place for you. The loss of awe is the great block to insight. A return to reverence is the first prerequisite for a

---

[19] Ibid., 25.
[20] Anthony Flew, *There is a God* (New York: HarperCollins, 2007), 181.

revival of wisdom, for the discovery of the world as an allusion to God. Wisdom comes from awe rather than from shrewdness. It is evoked not in moments of calculation but in moments of being in rapport with the mystery of reality. The greatest insights happen to us in moments of awe. A moment of awe is a moment of self-consecration. They who sense the wonder share in the wonder. They who keep holy the things that are holy shall themselves become holy.[21]

The word *awesome* is much overused and thereby reduced to being a label for almost any mundane matter. Heschel, of course, used it in the traditional sense to refer to what is "extremely daunting; inspiring great admiration, apprehension or fear." That the universe is truly most awesome can be confidently affirmed even when we experience our most agnostic moments.

Our awareness of this awesomeness of the universe can be obscured by the fact that it is in our everyday experience but if we do not have the sense of awe, we are missing

---

[21] Abraham Joshua Heschel, *God in Search of Man: A Philosophy of Judaism*. (New York: Farrar, Straus and Girouz, 1955), 77—78.

something real and vital. When awe is experienced, ordinary events can suddenly break through to us with a totally new type of awareness. These moments should be remembered and explored. The vivid new awareness may be of something very familiar—even what we think of as ordinary. We may suddenly ponder how a small seed can become a giant tree. A human egg and sperm join and a human results and at some point ponders in wonder at the mystery of existence. To fly across the expanse of the ocean can be a moment when a new awesomeness is deeply felt. To cross the ocean by ship can do this also. After three days seeing nothing but ocean and realizing I was only half way across, I was suddenly overwhelmed with a sense of the awesome size of the ocean.

The dimension of time can also break through as awesome. An anthropologist, Loren Eiseley, has written of his experience when making his way down an immense cliff, reaching a small opening and suddenly seeing an ancient, pre-historic skull staring back at him. This had once been a living being and Eiseley was suddenly overwhelmed with an awareness of the awesome dimension of time.[22] I vividly remember a moment at recess in the fourth grade when I became vividly aware that the world had existed for thousands of years—my time frame at that point—before I existed. It was not a new thought but I experienced it with a whole new vividness. As strange as such moments can feel, they are openings to levels of awareness that are valuable.

As already noted, science is an extremely valuable aid in making us aware of innumerable findings that can stimulate our awe. The world is not what it seems to be in everyday life. So much has been discovered that exists but that we cannot know it through any of our senses. The undoubtable foundation for us—the starting point—is a conscious recognition that we live in a universe that exists and is overwhelmingly awesome if we will but notice it. Its realms are both visible and invisible. We return to the philosopher's question, "Why is there something instead of nothing?" Can I accept that it is possible that in addition to the invisible world that physics now knows, there might be other invisible aspects? To ask again, is there any reason to not have an open mind about this?

_____

[22] Loren Eiseley, *The Immense Journey* (New York: Random House, 1957), 1—5.

We cannot doubt that the awesome universe exists and we cannot doubt that we exist. We also cannot doubt that existence had a cause. The idea that there must be an explanation for what exists is a deeply embedded assumption in all of the natural sciences. Where there are effects, there are causes. It is extremely difficult and maybe impossible to really think of matters that are uncaused. As the simple maxim claims, "If you see a turtle on top of a fencepost you know it didn't get there by itself."

Some people are suspicious of expressing that the origin of the universe was a creation. This seems to link it to some form of creationism that they reject. It is important not to get hung up on words and miss the reality that they identify. Whatever may be one's cosmology, the existence of the universe and our presence in it justifies that we consider it as a creation with a creator. If, as many believe, the universe is the random consequence of unguided processes, it is still a creation [i.e. the processes "created"] and has a creator [i.e. the process "created"]. Cosmology searches for this "creation" in natural processes. The religious quest also seeks to understand the origins of the universe and why it exists.

The Judeo-Christian tradition had no direct contact with the cause of the cosmos. The biblical accounts emerged *ex post facto*—long after the origin. What is important for the empirically minded is to understand that in the Bible it is the invisible creator that is designated as God. It is not that the biblical writers knew God and were then informed by this God that he was also the creator. Rather, they started—as do cosmologists—with the idea of a creating cause and explored to understand what that meant.

When Moses, according to the account, saw the burning bush and heard what he believed was a non-human voice, he immediately wanted to know the name of the speaker. "I am" was the response. (Exod. 3:14) This may seem like a curious statement but it is profound and profoundly important. It posits that the Hebrew reference to God is fundamentally a search for the reality of the universe. It asks what is the ultimate truth—God was the label that was used for what "is"—the "I am."

The ancient Hebrews pondered the creation and their experiences over a period of time and established their traditions. God was understood as the term to refer to the creator whatever or whoever the creator might be. When Abraham spoke of God he referred to him as "the Lord, God Most High, Creator of heaven and earth." (Gen. 14:22) The prophet, Isaiah, wrote, "Do you not know? Have you not heard? The Lord is the everlasting God, the Creator of the ends of the earth." (Isa. 40:28) It affirms that in Judeo-Christian religion God is what "is" and the universe is the effect of what "is." This concept of God represents the most fundamental reality—God is what is and what created the universe. Cosmology and religion are both in their own ways the search for the origin, the search for reality, the search for what is.

If the Judeo-Christian understanding of this Creator God, could be proven, neither the riddle nor the mystery would be eliminated. We would have to face the same question in a different form: "Who created God?" The physicist, Paul Davies, has stated that, "dumping the problem in the lap of a pre-existing designer is no explanation at all as it merely begs the question of who designed the designer." [23] Anthony Flew's response to the "who created the creator" question was: "If anything at all

---

[23] Paul Davies, "Yes, the universe looks like a fix. But that doesn't mean that a god fixed it." *The Guardian*, June 25, 2007.

exists, there must be something preceding it that always existed. . . Take your pick: God or universe. Something always existed."[24] Davies notes that scientists who explain the origin of the universe by, "appealing to a host of unseen universes and a set of unexplained meta-laws is scarcely any better."[25] The Nobel Prize winning physiologist, George Wald, has argued that to say "life arose spontaneously" is to "choose to believe the impossible."[26] Which of the impossible beliefs do we choose?

To accept the assumption that the universe had a cause leads to the question as to what are the characteristics of this cause. What is the "is"? John Polkinghorne, as has already been noted, proposed that both the religious search and science's cosmological search do not have direct observation and therefore cannot prove their theories. What both can do is assemble empirical facts— the knowable—and ask what theory best interprets these

---

[24] *There is a God*, 165. It should be noted that after publication there was some controversy over charges that some of the ideas in the book were from a co-author rather than Flew—a charge Flew vigorously denied.

[25] Quoted by John Humphreys in his book, *In God We Doubt* (London: Hodder & Stoughton, 2007, 48-9.

[26] Anthony Flew, *There is a God*, 131.

facts. The scientific search for truth utilizes the classic method of both inductive and deductive processes. The inductive stage looks for empirical data that is gathered and then analyzed to suggest possible theoretical explanations. When the theory has been developed, the deductive process is undertaken to test the theory. This approach is an empirically grounded method applicable to both cosmology and religion. This search for the best fit does not retreat into agnosticism and neither does it claim an unwarranted certainty. It advocates a careful examination of what we can know and a cautious but assertive examination of what theory best fits with reality.

It seems to me that most Christians follow only a deductive approach. They have "tried" the Christian religion and have found that it works for them. This sufficiently confirms for them the truthfulness of their faith. Most of the preaching and teaching I have read and heard in church takes this deductive approach. Christianity is believed to be true because it works. Billy Graham has described his faith in what is clearly the deductive approach. As a young man, he was filled with doubt and after wrestling with it he decided to put away doubt and try faith. He discovered that faith worked. His experience confirmed the hypothesis. Similarly, a young John Wesley wrestled with doubt but had what has been known as his Aldersgate experience in London in 1738 when his heart was "strangely warmed."

The questioning of the truth of Christianity is very old—as old as Christianity itself—and the deductive solution is also very old. Again, the truth of the hypothesis was confirmed by experience but it lacked empirical grounding.

I see no reason to criticize this approach but it is not satisfactory to the empirically minded because it does not include the inductive process. It is not empirically grounded. In the inductive approach, one gathers data—empirical information—and from this data emerges a theory that best reflects and is consistent with the data. The inductive grounding of that theory provides an empirical basis for confidence in a theory if it is confirmed. For the empirically minded, the deductive testing must be preceded by the most effective inductive process possible. Polkinghorne describes the inductive process as a "bottoms up" approach because it gathers real world "concrete" data from which to construct abstract theory.

As an example of the inductive process, I once supervised a graduate student thesis in which the student was studying the turnover rate of foster-care house parents. She examined the research literature and found that the high turnover rate had been found to be a result of burnout. In this research the theory of burnout was hypothesized without inductive evidence. The graduate student decided to look at this from the bottom-up inductive approach. She extensively interviewed former foster care house parents asking them to tell their own story without any direction from her. In doing this, she gathered observations from which to formulate a theory. What she found was that the former house parents had, indeed, experienced high stress in the job and this explained their answers but they had not burned out. They had taken the job with the intention of keeping it for only a short time. Most had gone from this job into other child-care and child-service employment. The inductive approach not only gave the graduate student new insights into foster house parenting, it revealed why the deductive research had confirmed the theory but had been mistaken. Yes, they had found the job tiring and difficult and this seemed to confirm the burnout theory but they had not experienced burnout. This thesis gave a better understanding because it used an inductive grounded approach.

The traditional Judeo-Christian understanding has been that there was a creation and the source of this can best be understood as from a mind that is in some way like a person.[27] However, no image of anything in heaven should be made. (Exod. 20:4) Humans cannot adequately conceptualize God and perhaps we do well to understand clearly that whatever mental images we have of God will be inadequate.

The empirical question is to consider if what is known could make the creation more likely the product of a mind or some non-mind process. I can only suggest a few ideas for what is an extensive but extremely important topic. For Polkinghorne, the answer is that the best fit to all that he knows is found in the hypothesis of a Creator Mind.

---

[27] There are several names in the Hebrew text that are translated as *God* but they share in the designation as the power of the Creator.

The earth seems more like the product of a mind than of a random uncaused phenomenon. He considers that the explanation of a creation from the assumption that an infinite number of multiple universes could produce the intricacies necessary for human life is much less probable.[28]

Polkinghorn's work is very helpful to me because he directly addresses the questions of Christian faith always working from a base of empiricism. His work as well as that of others reflect a variety of perspectives and all deserve careful consideration. My purpose here is only to identify these considerations. I do not expect this brief survey to be persuasive.

Anthony Flew wrote and debated for decades this question contending that the best fit for understanding the universe is atheism. After long defending this position, he became persuaded that the universe seemed much more likely to be the product of a mind rather than impersonal, random causes. His perspective evolved in response to the work of many scientists and much reflection. While it is unfair to characterize these influences in a few words,

---

[28] *Science and Religion in the Quest of Truth*, 70—78.

it is interesting to briefly and superficially note three of the points he has cited. These were DNA, the "monkey theorem," and reflections on the concept of natural law. Concerning DNA he wrote, "What I think the DNA material has done is that it has shown, by the almost unbelievable complexity of the arrangements which are needed to produce (life), that intelligence must have been involved in getting these extraordinarily diverse elements to work together. It's the enormous complexity of the numbers of elements and the enormous subtlety of the ways they work together."[29]

A strange but interesting influence to Flew was Gerry Schroeder's "point by point refutation" of the "monkey theorem." This theorem is the idea that "defends the possibility of life arising by chance using the analogy of a multitude of monkeys banging away on computer keyboards and eventually ending up writing a Shakespearean sonnet." This theorem is a metaphor for the notion that the universe is so large and time so extended in the billions of years that life could have spontaneously emerged. Strange as it seems, the British

---

[29] *There is a God*, 74—75.

National Council of Arts actually put six monkeys in a cage with a computer for a month. They produced fifty pages but not a single word. Schroeder calculated that the odds for producing a single word to be one in 27,000. He calculated on the number of protons in the universe and if "you turn the entire universe into these microcomputer chips and these chips were spinning a million times a second [producing] letters, the number of trials you would get since the beginning of time . . . You will never get a sonnet by chance."[30]

Is this serious scientific exploration? Flew found Schroeder's research careful and persuasive. Projecting onto the universe an explanation of chance natural processes became unconvincing. He cited physicist Paul Davies, "The problem of how meaningful or semantic information can emerge spontaneously from a collection of mindless molecules subject to blind and purposeless forces presents a deep conceptual challenge."[31] The "monkey theorem" has been around for a long time but only as a thought. Schroeder actually ran a test to evaluate it.

---

[30] Ibid., 75—77.
[31] Ibis., 129.

Flew also was much influenced by reflecting on the fact that science has discovered laws of nature that can be described through rational analysis and expressed mathematically. He cites Paul Davies again: "How is it that we have a set of laws that drives feature-less gases to life, consciousness and intelligence?[32] We do discover these laws—regularities—and they can be expressed in rational mathematical equations. The correspondence of the natural world and the rational world came to profoundly influence his perspective. Polkinghorne expresses it through a quote of Eugene Wigner, "Why is mathematics so unreasonably effective?" Polkinghorn explained, "Mathematics—that most abstract of disciplines—which time and again has provided the key to unlocking the secrets of the physical universe."[33]

It is not only that the universe exists, but also that we know that it exists. Flew notes that, "Today there is a growing awareness of awareness. We are conscious and conscious that we are conscious . . . The problem becomes insoluble when you realize the nature of neurons. First of all, neurons show no resemblance to our conscious life.

[32] Ibid., 108.
[33] *Science and Religion in the Quest for Truth*, 72—73.

Second and more importantly, their physical properties do not in any way give reason to believe that they can or will produce consciousness." It is both the evidence that the universe seems to be an expression of mind and that our consciousness is an inexplicable product of the creation." [34]

These are ideas to ponder. They represent grounded observations that can be organized to see what "best fits" with theories of both cosmology and Christianity. I am not qualified to speak for science and make no claim how these views would fare if all scientists were polled on the issue. What is persuasive is that there are excellent scientists who believe that a verisimilitudinous case for a minded creation is not only plausible but is more likely.

The starting point is that we exist and existence had a cause. An aspect of our existence is that we are minded animals—we are aware that we exist. We are aware that we are aware. Therefore we ponder the question of the origin and meaning. In Moses' concept, the creator was God and God is what "is". The question becomes, is this

---

[34] *There is a God,* 173—174.

"is" more likely to have been something like a mind? Or, is it a result of some non-minded cause? What is this invisible creator like? Is there any evidence that can take us beyond Moses' definition that God is what is? That we exist and we sense that our existence seems in some sense to indicate a causal mind, does not give us a link to Christian explanations. It also does not rule them out and that linkage must be pursued.

Chapter

3

Is the Universe Friendly?

*E*ven if there were persuasive evidence that the universe is best understood as a product of mind, this would not tell us what the characteristics of that mind might be. Philosophers have sometimes phrased this question, "Is the universe friendly?" That is, does the mind of the Creator know us? Does the Creator care? Is the mind malevolent? Or, is the mind friendly toward humanity? Are there grounded empirical factors that are verisimilitudeness? That is, what do we know and what fits best to indicate what we have no way of knowing. Is the universe friendly?

The Jewish and Christian belief is that God is not only friendly but also loving. The covenant between God and the Jews was a covenant of love. (Deut.7:9) The New Testament has the declaration that, "God is love." (1 John 4:8, 16) Are there any empirical grounds to support this? If, as many believe, the universe operates only by the regularities of "natural law" then the universe would seem to be indifferent to human well-being. Even if there was a Creator God, it is certainly possible that this God would be indifferent to human existence. It is also possible that the universe could have originated by a malevolent Creator.

The universe can certainly seem indifferent to human well-being. Phenomena such as the law of gravity or the sunrise seem to operate with invariability no matter what humans think. Science assumes that the real world operates on the basis of regularity—that is by "natural law"—and this assumption has been fruitful in producing a vast array of scientific applications. Jesus spoke of this regularity when he observed, "[God] causes the sun to rise on the evil and the good, and sends rain on the righteous and unrighteous." (Matt. 5:45)

The term, *natural law*, though conventional, does not refer to a law. Rather, it refers to observed regularities in the natural world. The regularities are the way things seem to be but there is no law. This regularity of natural law seems to be a verisimilitudinous fit for the hypothesis that the universe operates by its own regularities and is indifferent to human well-being. The regularity of the natural world can seem to indicate a Creator who is indifferent or at least is not active in human experience.

The universe of nature can certainly seem also to be indifferent to human well-being when we are in the midst of natural disasters. It does not seem friendly when we consider the predatory behavior of the animal kingdom's "tooth and claw." The universe does not seem friendly when we look at human-caused disasters where human animosity expresses itself by inflicting unimaginable suffering. There are so many places and times where existence is exceedingly painful and in which there is no relief from the suffering. Why would a caring Mind permit this? When this is the world people experience, the hypothesis that the "universe is friendly" seems very flawed. The interpretation that the universe is at best indifferent if not malevolent can then seem to fit reality—to be verisimilitudinous. The unnecessary but very real, extensive, and chronic human suffering is perhaps the most difficult challenge to the assertion by Christians that God is love. It is referred to as *theodicy* and theologians and philosophers have wrestled with this for centuries. The overwhelming suffering for so many remains a challenge to Christian claims that God is love. This challenge must not be ignored in any consideration of the nature of the Creator.

There are, however, some important indicators that suggest that the universe can be considered to be friendly. First, it is not a matter to be ignored that life can be experienced as very good. The universe can be a place of exquisite happiness. When it is good we may sense that the "powers that be"—if there are such—are working in our favor. When we are healthy and safe with good food and shelter, life can be experienced as good. Whether this makes us happy is more complicated. The universe can seem to coalesce as an environment where we can flourish. When that is our experience, we may believe we are in a human-friendly universe. This experience could seem to confirm the reality of a friendly and loving God.

This does not prove that the universe is "friendly" but

it does recognize the existence of a creation that can be favorable to human experience. The book of Job tells us that Satan argued that Job had served God because his life had experienced only good times. Satan charged that Job served God because God had "put a hedge around him" and had given him a good life. "Strike everything he has and he will surely curse you to your face," Satan told God. (Job 1:9—11). Yet, even in overwhelming suffering, Job refused to curse God. Why would this be the case? Perhaps, even in extremity people can perceive a sense of the "good." Satan's observation, however, is important. When life is good it can make sense of experience to believe that the "universe is friendly." When life is chronic suffering, it poses for the Christian the opposite issue as to how to reconcile a loving God and human suffering. The point to be made here is that both human suffering and human well-being are real. For all that humans suffer, the world is also a place where humans can be happy. This potential for happiness should also be considered as part of the human experience.

A second consideration that indicates a friendly universe is the anthropic principle. This is a science-based hypothesis interpreting that the existence of life as we know it requires such an intricate combination of features that it is unlikely—even impossible—that it could have happened by chance. Polkinghorne has observed that "evolution by itself is not enough to produce fruitfulness; it has to operate in a suitably 'finely tuned' natural environment."[35] This universe must be immense, he noted, to create the forces to support life so that it could evolve and there must be "astonishing specificity" for the carbon-based life we know. There must also be a flexibility such as has been found in quantum mechanics to "give the balance between stability and openness" for life to evolve.[36] This view argues that there must have been purpose in creation. Polkinghorne holds that it is "a fact of interest calling for an explanation."[37] The anthropic principle suggests a level of "friendliness" in the sense that the created universe seems to have been intentionally formed for a planet that supports life and human existence.

Antony Flew, the already cited philosopher of science

---

[35] *Scientists as Theologians* (London:SCPK, 1996) 50—52.
[36] *Faith, Science and Understanding* (New Haven: Yale University Press), 68, 86
[37] *Scientists as Theologians*, 52.

and long-time atheist, has written about his change of perspective to theism. In this he commented, "If one of the fundamental constants—the speed of light or the mass of an electron, for instance—had been to the slightest degree different, then no planet capable of permitting the evolution of human life could have formed."[38] Flew gives as an analogy that if he checked into a hotel and upon entering saw a framed print identical to one he had at home, his favorite music playing, and his favorite cookies on the table, he would assume that someone knew he was coming to that hotel. He quotes a physicist, Freeman Dyson, who has written, "The more I examine the universe and study the details of its architecture the more evidence I find that the universe in some sense knew we were coming."[39] The anthropic principle is an interpretation that supports the idea of a friendly universe.

A third indicator that the universe may be friendly is found in our capacity for and need for human friendship. Meaningful companionship is a crucial factor contributing to the quality of our lives. Again and again, athletes say that it was the team experience that was the

---

[38] Flew, Antony, *There is a God* (New York: HarperColins, 2007), 115.
[39] Ibid, 113—114.

highlight of their sports experience. The human animal needs human friendship—indeed, was designed for it. Whether our experiences of friendship fulfills us or leaves us with a degree of loneliness and disappointment, the fact is that the universe is friendly in the sense that human friendship is an important and an enriching experience.

As humans, we are minded—we have self-awareness of ourselves, our past experiences, and what we anticipate in the future including death. We ponder what our existence and the universe might mean. What we think about these matters crucially effects our lives. The Bible's classic statement declares, "[God] has also set eternity in the hearts of men; yet no one can fathom what God has done from beginning to end." (Eccles. 3:11) Is being a minded individual—conscious of these aspects—a sign of a "friendly" universe or an evolutionary mutation without significance?

Why do we have this capacity for self-awareness and reflection? Why do we wonder about our world and think about the possibility of God. Why do we think that there could be a God who cares about us? The psalmist asked of God, "What is mankind that you are mindful of them?" (Ps. 8:4) Job posed it also, "What is mankind that you make so much of them, that you give them so much attention? (Job 7:17) The question is repeated in the New Testament. (Heb. 2:6) The capacity for friendship and the enrichment of experience it provides can be an indicator of a Creator's mind that is friendly.

The Judeo-Christian claim that God is a loving creator does not include the claim that human experience will always reflect this. Mother Theresa, we have learned, for all of her works and commitment experienced periods when God seemed absent. The Bible deals with both a sense of the presence of God and the absence of God. Unfortunately, churches tend to speak only of presence. Numerous Psalms as well as other passages deal with the sense of God as absent, distant, and unresponsive. For examples the psalmist speaks to these words to God,

> Why, Lord, do you stand far off? Why do you hide yourself in times of trouble? (Ps. 10:1)

> How long, Lord? Will you forget me forever? How long will you hide your face from me? (Ps. 13:1)

> You have taken from me friend and neighbor; the darkness is my closest friend. (Ps. 88:18.)

> My God, I cry out by day but you do not answer. (Ps. 22:2)

As has been already noted, Jesus' cry from the cross was that God had forsaken him. (Mark 15:34) A sense that God is absent can be part of the spiritual experience. Despite the sense of God's friendly presence that many experience, God remains hidden. It is a crucial step to assess the possibility that the universe can be understood as a product of a friendly Creator. We can affirm that, no matter what is encountered, the world is a place where life can be very good. The anthropic theory holds that this is not an illusion or gloss but reflects the very intricacies of the whole universe as prepared for human existence. We know that the human experience includes the capacity for friendship as a real and meaningful experience. These form a basis for considering the verisimilitudinous hypothesis that the universe does reflect a mind that is friendly. Puzzles still remain. Many questions are unanswered but these need not negate the reality that there are reasons to believe that the universe is friendly.

This chapter has begun to examine if there is a link between the Creator and the Judeo-Christian interpretation of that Creator. The links discussed so far between the origin of the universe and a friendly God, are tenuous. Fortunately, there are other factors that can strengthen this linkage.

Chapter

4

The God Who Talks

To accept the possibility, as advocated by some philosophers and scientists, that the universe seems to have been the product of a mind does not mean that this mind is also God as understood by Christians. Whether there is such a link between creation and the Christian religion has not yet been addressed here. When the Israelites left their slavery in Egypt, they fled into the desert and there they asked, "Is the Lord among us or not?" (Exod. 17:7) This is still the question. Is there any evidence that the mind that created the world is interactive with humans as believed by Christians?

The Christian claim is that the Mind who created the universe is the God of the Bible and this God communicates with humans. This God is with us. God has spoken. God talks. This is the link and by itself it undoubtedly seems tenuous and probably not persuasive. It is where we will start. It will take more words than it would seem to warrant because it is tenuous and easily dismissed. Once understood, however, it will lead into other important linkages.

From beginning to end, the Christian Bible is the story of the Creator God who speaks to people in words, visions, and dreams. In the beginning of Genesis, God talks to Adam and Eve. In the last book, Revelation, John records in detail a vision he saw of heaven. In between are accounts such as that of a Gentile named Cornelius who saw an angel and heard the angel's voice. At the same time, Peter had a dream in which he received the message to meet with Cornelius. In his dream Peter learned that he was to extend the Christian message to the Gentiles and that was to transform Christianity from being a Jewish religion to one that included Gentiles as well as Jews. (Acts 10) Peter later recounted this experience in order to convince the Jewish Christians to accept this new inclusive practice. (Acts 11) These accounts of revelation convey the belief that the Creator is a God who communicates.

The definitive biblical statement is that God has communicated with humans at "many times and in various ways." (Heb. 1:1—2) It does not claim that this is common. It does not claim that such communication is necessary or that it is a sign that one is a Christian but it does claim that God has communicated and therefore it can be said that, "the Lord is among us." It accepts the Jewish tradition that God spoke to Moses and others. It posits that the most complete communication was through Jesus who personified the Creator God. There were also occasions in Jesus' life where there were explicit dreams, visions, and voices. (Matt.3:16; 17:1—6) These were considered to be evidence that God was among them.

Daniel Smith has made a careful scientifically oriented study of what he calls, "auditory hallucinations." This term refers to the experience of hearing a voice when no one is present.[40] His study originated in a personal interest and not a religious quest. He had never heard voices himself but became interested in the subject when he discovered a written document from his grandfather

---

[40] Daniel B. Smith, *Muses, Madmen, and Prophets* (New York: Penguin Group, 2007), 1-5.

who had regularly heard voices over many years. His grandfather had listened to the voices and found them to be very helpful except when he had tried to use them to bet on horses. He had kept his experience of voices as a secret but when Daniel's father learned of it, he became very angry. He also had heard voices and was terrified by the voices, as he believed they indicated he was developing a mental illness. Although he had not become mentally ill, he had lived many years in secret terror that he would. Neither had spoken of this to others. The father was angry that his father—Smith's grandfather—had never told him. To keep such experiences a secret and to fear that it is a symptom of illness is understandable. To tell about such an experience would risk being identified as mentally ill in contemporary culture.

While it is true that a characteristic of some mental illness is to hear voices that can be thought to be from God, Smith has documented that voices, visions and revealing dreams also can occur to very healthy people. Sometimes they are thought to be communications from God but often they are simply puzzling or disturbing experiences as in the cases of Smith's father and grandfather.

A book by a sociologist and priest, Andrew Greeley, found in reviewing empirical studies that many people had had experiences they considered to be direct contact with God.[41] Both Greeley and Smith discovered that while many people have had such experiences, few have talked about it. Many neither anticipated the voices nor did they necessarily welcome them. They did not make claims or boast about it. They only confirmed that it had happened.

The notion of God speaking in dreams has never been of particular interest to me even though I have had two dreams that seemed to be totally different from all of the other dreams I have experienced. What seemed clear in both dreams was a sense of having received a message. Could it have been from God? I have never claimed that it was and would not. If a dream instructed me to do something that I knew to be wrong I would totally discount it. I only know that each of the two dreams was a totally different experience from conventional dreams.

In his research, Smith noted that what he called the "divine voice speaks profoundly in the history of Christianity." He traced this from the early church fathers

---

[41] *The Sociology of the Paranormal: A Reconnaissance* (Beverly Hills: Sage Publications, 1975)

to the poets John Milton and William Blake. He wrote, "The divine voice runs like a trail through Christian history. And then, it seems, the trail runs cold." He continued, "Somewhere around the eighteenth century, the culture's way of thinking and talking about unusual experiences altered markedly. What was once revelation and inspiration became symptom and pathology."[42]

Smith's interpretation seems to me to be both correct and incorrect. The culture did shift as he noted but it did not entirely run cold. There have continued to be many Christians who believe they have discerned the voice of God and today there are many claims by people that God has spoken to them. Some Christian denominations encourage this sense that God communicates with individuals but other denominations do not.

Anthropologist T. M. Luhrmann studied a church that encouraged the sense of experiencing a presence of God and hearing God speak.[43] They were very careful to critically examine what they had heard. Many members had never had such experience and these were not thought

---

42 *Muses, Madmen, and Prophets*, 13-14.
43 *When God Talks Back*, (New York: Alfred A. Knopf, 2012)

lesser of for not having had them. They did not boast or make claims.

Pat Robertson, on the other hand, has become notorious for claims such as the one that God told him why Hurricane Katrina devastated much of New Orleans. There are books such as *Conversations with God* that portray what are claimed to be literal conversations of speaking and hearing that occurred between God and the author.[44] Candidates for the United States Presidency sometimes have claimed that God told them to run for the office. Ryan Hall trained and competed in the 2012 Olympics using God as his coach. He based his unorthodox preparation on what he experienced that God was telling him to do. There are still reports of voices being heard.

The contemporary claim to have heard God speak, however, is for many Christians not acceptable because they believe that God stopped communicating after the age of the Apostles. For them, claims to have heard God speak such as those made by Pat Robertson are necessarily dismissed as bogus. They do believe that God

---

[44] Neale Donald Walsch, *The Complete Conversations with God* (New York: G P Putnam's Sons, 2005). This includes all three books in the series.

communicated in the past as recorded in the Bible and for them this is sufficient. It should be noted that there is no biblical text that indicates that God would stop speaking.

The claim that "God told me" to do something " is usually made without an explicit description of what exactly happened. I do not recall that any of the presidential candidates who claimed that God told them to run have described the experience of discerning God's voice. It would seem that many such claims of communication are not direct and specific such as those Pat Robertson has claimed but reflect a spiritual experience in which a dream, a prayer, or a meditation results in a convincing sense that God would want one to take a certain action.

Sometimes the sense of a communication can be very vague. William Wordsworth's poem, for example, written near Tintern Abbey expresses this, "I have felt a presence that disturbs me with the joy of elevated thoughts; a sense sublime of something far more deeply interfused." For others, the sense of a communication received has clear, specific ideas.

Biblical accounts also exhibit a range. For Elijah, it was a "gentle whisper." (1 Kings 19:12) For Isaiah, it was dramatic and visual as well as auditory. He saw "the Lord" with seraphs flying and smoke filling the temple. He heard a voice calling him to become a prophet and he committed himself to do so. (Isa. 6:1—10) Joan of Arc in the fifteenth century heard voices telling her to lead the army and overthrow the enemies of France. She was a peasant girl with no military experience but she obeyed the voices she referred to as her "counsel" and instructed the French generals how to throw out the British. She succeeded but by 1431 she had been captured by the English, tried, and burned as a heretic. The issue at her trial was neither whether she had heard voices nor whether she was mentally ill. She was tried on the charges to determine whether the voices she heard were from God or from the Devil.[45]

What should we make of the claims about having heard voices, having seen visions and having had revelatory dreams? I appreciate very much that I was not taught as a child to believe that ghosts and curses were considered real. When the "evil eye" was believed to be real, people

---

[45] See chapter 10 in *Muses, Madmen, and Prophets* for an account of Joan of Arc's life and situation.

suffered much when they thought they were under a curse. I appreciate liberation from these superstitions considered in the past to be real and powerful. I do not want to be gullible to superstitious claims. When someone announces that God has told him to take some action, I do not simply assume that it is true.

My commitment to empiricism and science, however, requires that an open mind is in order. Whatever hearing voices means, these are reports of human experience. As such, they are data. To dismiss all such claims whether as symptoms of mental illness or weakness is not warranted unless, in fact, these are conclusions based on an examination of evidence. We should be skeptical of claims to have heard God speak but skepticism is not a sufficient reason to deny the reality that this phenomenon of voices and visions exists. The fact that I have never heard a voice does not mean that it has not happened. The fact that there are widespread reports is evidence of a phenomenon to be investigated whatever it may mean.

Furthermore, reports of having heard voices are not found only in Christianity. Mohammad claimed that he was visited by an angel. The ancient author, Homer, in *The Iliad* and *The Odyssey* reported many communications from the gods. Socrates heard a voice that he considered his muse. Joseph Smith, the founder of Mormonism received communications not recognized by mainstream Christianity.

What does it mean for Christians if it is claimed that non-Christians also hear voices? One theme of Jesus' teaching was that God had spoken to people of other religions and not only to Jews. Once, when Jesus spoke about this in his hometown, people who had just praised his wise teaching became so outraged at his claim that they tried to kill him. (Luke 4:14-29)

For many Christians today, the idea that God may have spoken to the Buddha or to Mohammad is still extremely troublesome—so much so that it may seem to be wrong to even consider it. If this causes outrage, it is the same response as that which Jesus encountered though hopefully without the violence. There is an important question in this to ponder: Could not the Creator God have spoken to Buddha or anyone God would choose? Could not God have revealed to such people a different set of ideas from what was given in the Judeo-Christian tradition? This changes nothing about the idea that God has spoken in Christianity.

To counter this, one verse of Scripture is inevitably mentioned. When Peter and John appeared before Annas, the High Priest and declared, "Salvation is found in no one else, for there is no other name under heaven given to mankind by which we must be saved." (Acts 4:12) This was stated to people who were hearing Peter's testimony. Any interpretation of this passage should also consider what Paul wrote concerning those who did not know the Jewish and Christian message. Those who did not know this message were not to be judged on the basis of what they did not know but on what they did know—their own religious understanding. (Rom. 2:14—16)[46]

It is interesting that while there are many claims in the New Testament that God has spoken, the New Testament does not make the claim that its own writings are themselves the word of God. In Luke's Gospel he claimed that his writing was the product of careful research. (1:1—4) The book of Revelation is a writing of a vision of

---

[46] I have explored this question in more detail in *Two Different Worlds*, (Newark: University of Deleware Press, 1988,) chapter 9.

heaven. The other New Testament writings report voices, visions, and dreams that are from God but they do not give any mention as to the circumstances of the writing of the documents themselves. Even though the New Testament does not claim itself to be a direct revelation, it does describe voices, visions, and dreams that are believed to be revelations. It is not the writings but Jesus who is identified in the text as the Word of God. (John 1:1—14) The Bible is the record of many revelations through voices, visions, and dreams which in the aggregate contain the experiences that compose and communicate the Jewish and Christian traditions.

The Jewish Scriptures were regarded by Jesus and the Apostles as authoritative. Paul referred to them as "holy" and "God breathed."(2 Tim. 3:15—16) The New Testament writings have also been received as authoritative for Christians. These are the writings that give us direct access to what the early Christians expressed about the life of Jesus and the Christian faith. My point here is to note what the documents do and do not claim for themselves—they do not claim to be themselves the direct revelation but they report events that they believed were direct revelation.

The writings that make up the Christian Bible are the compositions of many people over many centuries that are for Christians the authoritative record. They are the record of the voices, visions, and dreams as well as teachings and events that are fundamental to Christianity. The Bible never suggests that to be a Christian one should have heard the voice of God. It does not say that those who do are superior to those who do not. It does not suggest that voices should be heard with regularity. My conclusion is that hearing voices is a widespread and longstanding phenomenon that while not unique to Christianity, is central in the development of the Christian faith.

There were experiences of revelation such as the aforementioned dreams of Peter and Cornelius that were accepted as revelation and in that acceptance, the direction of the church was altered. What seems clear is that the early church accepted revelation through voices, visions, and dreams but it was not dependent upon it. They did not emphasize it. They did not expect it. They did not wait for it. The church focused on the life and teachings of Jesus and of the Apostles. That voices could occur was accepted but they were not necessary for the normal operations of the early Christians. Even in the discussion of accepting Gentiles into the church, James referred to the "signs and wonders" but sought to persuade by contending on the basis of his own judgment in the matter. (Acts 15:19)

If we accept that personal revelation such as the voices can be God speaking, would this not create much confusion? How can we judge the legitimacy of such claims? The New Testament attests to complications such as when Simon who was a sorcerer wanted to buy the Holy Spirit to add to his trade. (Acts 8:9—25) Paul warned against deceiving spirits and false apostles. (2 Cor. 11:12—15; 1 Tim.4:1) Christians were never encouraged to accept claims of revelation uncritically.

Perhaps the best commentary on dealing with confusion was the experience of the early church in Corinth. What was called "speaking in tongues"—a work of the Spirit of God—was occurring and was creating conflict. (1 Cor. 12-15) Paul established guidelines noting that God is not a god of "disorder but of peace. (1 Cor. 14:33) While Paul accepted revelation including what had been involved in his own conversion experience, he was very explicit to the Corinthians that such revelation was less important than the central gospel theme of love. To make this clear, he wrote the words so often quoted as the "love chapter" that are recorded in 1 Corinthians 13. He was explicit that people differ in their abilities and experiences and that one who has heard a "supernatural" voice is not superior to one who has not.

What seems clear to me is that both sides in the issue about voices can be true. The early church had experiences of voices, visions, and dreams that were accepted as revelation. But it is also true that the church operated on the basis of their understanding of Christ and the apostle's teaching rather than on extensive use of revelations. When Apollos was mistaken in his teaching, it was Priscilla and Acquila who taught him. (Acts 18:24—28) Not having had a voice to guide him was not considered to be a spiritual deficiency—he just had a lack of information.

Every social organization has a culture that has developed through a history of interaction. A culture is a defining tradition for the society. It will evolve out of the past experiences and express itself in its encounter with its present circumstances. The process of developing a culture is sometimes referred to as traditionalization. The Bible, in these terms, is a product of the Christian traditionalization. That is, it is the record of interactions among people who at times received communications they believed came from God. The sum of all experiences—both of revelation and non-revelation—evolved into the tradition that became the culture of Christianity.

The life of Jesus was pivotal in gaining a new perspective on the traditions of the Jews in his time. His life and teachings were integrated into the Jewish cultural traditions and with the interactions of the early Christians became the Christian tradition. To do this meant that Jesus had to live, interact with his disciples, and have them integrate all of these experiences into the life—the tradition—that was the early church.

If I were to hear what might be the voice of God, I would only consider it in the context of this centuries old tradition of the Judeo-Christian faith. Still, there is no reason to rule it out as totally impossible other than from a pre-determined conclusion. Not every voice is from God. Interpreting voices must be carefully considered.

There are readily available alternative explanations for the claim that God has spoken. As already noted, hearing voices can be a symptom of mental illness but it also occurs to people who are very healthy. Accompanied by other symptoms that indicate illness, the medical needs should be accepted and appropriate treatment applied. In the absence of other symptoms, there is no reason to assume that the voices are indicators of illness.

What really happens when healthy individuals hear voices? If we are persuaded that it cannot be the voice of a muse or of God, then all reports are wrong. If it cannot happen, it did not happen. The problem with this is that this is not empirical. It is in itself an act of faith—the faith that we know it cannot happen. If people report that it happened even though it cannot happen, the search is to find what did happen. Psychological explanations have been offered such as that it can be a defense mechanism against anxiety or perhaps a matter of hyper-suggestibility. Smith's search of the literature did not find a correlation that would account for the phenomenon of voices. While some seek to make use of the claim of voices for profit or power, the majority of people do not. Most ponder it and tell no one.

Many people, of course, have a desire to believe and some may grasp for what seems to validate their faith. Even here, the experience varies. Some people have a desire for unbelief as well. C. S. Lewis wrote of his own struggle in which he resisted faith only to give up, accept that he believed and then discovered that he was "surprised by joy."[47] Wishful thinking can work in both directions. To reduce the varieties of human experience to a simple human anxiety or wishful thinking without evidence is a reductionism that is uninformative. It does not account for the many manifestations of the phenomena.

A brief aside to consider is that in addition to the phenomenon of hearing voices there is what has come to be called the "near death experience." It shares with voices the fact that these are experiences that are not considered possible in a naturalistic culture except as some form of mental delusion or superstition. Nevertheless, the near death experience that seems to suggest that death could be a passage into another world has been recorded and analyzed for several decades. Raymond Moody first

---

[47] C. S. Lewis wrote an autobiographical book that he entitled, *Surprised by Joy*. (1955, Orlando: Harcourt Brace and Company)

published his work, *Life After Life*, in 1975. He and others have continued to gather accounts, analyze them and publish their findings.[48]

What grounded empirical conclusions can we make about the voices? They have been experienced by many people and thus are an empirical phenomenon to be explained. It is possible that hearing a voice is a symptom of mental illness. It is possible that it may be a result of some psychological need. It may be that one is in a church culture that teaches its members to expect to hear voices. These can account for some voices but they do not seem to me to be adequate explanations for the phenomenon. The widespread phenomena call for an open mind.

In the New Testament we read that Saul, the persecutor of Christians, was traveling to Damascus when he suddenly saw a bright light, fell to the ground, heard Jesus speak to him, and found that he had become blind. (Acts 9, 22, 26) We cannot know if God had blinded Saul of Tarsus. We cannot know if there was a mental illness involved. We also cannot claim to know that

---

[48] Raymond Moody, *Life After Life*, 1975; *Paranormal*, 2012; *Glimpses of Eternity*, 2010, *Coming Back*, 1995.

there was. Authors are not persuasive just because they claim to have heard the voice of God. The evidence of such widespread experiences, however, goes beyond the prevalent explanations. Reports of these phenomena are well established in human experience. They exist. There may be more to this than meets the eye—or ear. If it were only an account of Saul, we would and should be skeptical. The extensive occurrences of such phenomena call for more than skepticism. It makes a case for careful examination.

My guarded conclusion is that the phenomena of voices, revelatory dreams, and visions have been reported over many centuries and in many places. One collection of such experiences is found in the ancient Jewish tradition and writings. Growing from this tradition came the experiences that gave rise to the Christian tradition as recorded in the New Testament documents. The New Testament is the authoritative collection of these experiences coupled with the events that gave rise to the Christian faith.

We do not want to be gullible and we have good reason to be suspicious of claims to have heard a voice from God.

This is not ordinary, every day, empirical experience but it is a widespread phenomenon. Empiricism calls for an open mind and a willingness to search for evidence. It is the basic process by which claims for contact with God— the Creator Mind—have been made. It is a tenuous link and by itself is not persuasive. Fortunately, there are other factors to consider. The question is still pertinent: "Is the Lord among us?"

Chapter

5

Religious Experience

*J*f God talks to humans, those who hear him—in whatever way they "hear"—will have had a type of religious experience. The renowned philosopher, Elton Trueblood, published a book, *The Knowledge of God* in 1939 that called for an empirical approach to the study of religion. He contended that his "mood [was] . . . the mood of science, but [the] datam [was] the datum of religion."[49] It is empirically demonstrable that many people report such experiences in some form such as a sense of presence, a voice, a vision, or a dream.

The datum to which Trueblood referred was religious experience by which he meant what people reported as impressions of internal events that are religious. Trueblood

---

[49] *The Knowledge of God* (New York: Harper and Brothers, 1939), 28.

understood that for many people "religious experience is usually rejected as having no evidential value and no demonstrable objective reference."[50] It is dismissed for being subjective. Nevertheless, he contended, it exists and as such should be carefully considered: "To take it seriously does not mean to take it in blind faith, but rather as something demanding careful interpretation."[51]

Trueblood believed there was a record of subjective religious experience and that it was valid to consider objective. As a Quaker, he had been very involved in a tradition that valued quiet reflection on experience and whose members also wrote much about those experiences. His claim for indicators of an "objective order" came out of extensive experience and from studying documents not only from Quakers but also from other cultural and historical writings. He concluded about religious experience that though there are "obvious differences . . . they refer chiefly to matters of organization and liturgical details . . . and to differences of creed." However, "When we concentrate on the actual record of experience we are struck with the great degree of convergence in the

---

[50] Ibid., 10.
[51] Ibid., 12.

testimony." He added, "It is not strictly true that all the saints tell the same story, but it is true that they tell so nearly the same story that it is irrational not to suppose they are talking about the same objective order."[52] He compared the study of religious experience to looking through a microscope. To the uninitiated, one does not really know what is being seen but with cultivation of ability, the reality can be clearly delineated.[53] It was out of extensive study of accounts of religious experience that a commonness of experience becomes evident.

Religious experience is subjective in that it is an individual experience but in that it has similarities among people of diverse backgrounds, there is evidence of objectivity. To reject entirely the study of human experience because it is subjective would lead to a cessation of the study of many important subjects. Research on topics such as marriage, work organization, and voting behavior are three of many examples. Self-reporting of subjective experience is involved but correlation of experience variables can produce valuable objective findings. Such studies are referred to as "soft" because they must rely

---

[52] Ibid., 105—106.
[53] Ibid., 141—142.

on self-reporting of subjective experience but with an adaptation of methodology they have had proven value. The methodological issues must be encountered but this does not warrant discounting the adapted empirical scientific criteria.

"The primary datum of religion," Trueblood wrote, "may be stated as follows: Millions of men and women, throughout several thousand years, representing various races and nations, and including all levels of education or cultural opportunity, have reported an experience of God as the spiritual companion of their souls."[54] That most people do not report such experiences does not negate those who do have such experience. That such are reported over time and around the world is empirically established. The issue is what the experiences mean.

Religious experience is considered to be ineffable. This means that it is something that cannot be adequately expressed in human words. Trueblood notes that it is, "really ineffable [but] paradoxically, men like [George] Fox say, on the one hand, that what they know is inexpressible,

---

[54] Ibid., 11.

while on the other hand, they use volumes of print in the effort to do what they have said cannot be done."[55]

Trueblood added that "ineffability faces us constantly" in many areas of experience and is not unique to religion. He noted, "One has only to watch the efforts of a lover of music, as he tries to tell the unmusical about his experiences to realize that this is true. All the musical devotee can do is to use words of vivid imagery, which probably appear, to the unmusical hearer, vague, rhapsodical and largely meaningless." Trueblood added, "A somewhat humorous illustration of ineffability is provided in the experience of an academic friend who tried to tell a group of young persons about the joys of study. They could understand the need of study, but not its joy.[56]

Religious experience is real experience that being ineffable must be expressed in analogous imagery. As just noted, music is real and we can be deeply moved by it yet it also is ineffable and that is why we can tell so little about it.[57] The mythic imagery of religious expression should not be troublesome but recognized as the human

---

[55] Ibid., 82—83.
[56] Ibid., 83.
[57] Ibid., 85.

expression of ineffable experience. As it is ineffable, it must use imagery.

Trueblood stated that religious experience is perceptual, cognitive, and personal.[58] That is, those who experience it consider that it is real and an individualized event. It is found throughout time and around the world. It is significant in the lives of many individuals and has significant impact in society. There is no reason to ignore it or demean it. Rather, there is solid reason to critically and systematically examine it with the best empirical analysis possible.

There are variations in the way denominations define and practice religious experience. T. M. Luhrmann, an already mentioned anthropologist, authored an important book entitled: *When God Talks Back: Understanding the American Evangelical Relationship with God.*[59] What she found did not fit many popular stereotypes of religious experience. The evangelical Christians she studied gave central emphasis to developing a direct, active relationship

---

[58] Ibid., 65,71,73.
[59] *When God Talks Back: Understanding the American Evangelical Relationship with God* (New York: Alfred Knopf, 2012).

with God in which one could feel the presence and hear the voice of God. She wrote of these Christians, "The problem at the center of their faith is identifying the divine in ordinary life and distinguishing it from madness, evil, and simple human folly."[60] They did not take their experiences as genuine without giving them careful consideration and critical evaluation. Many members never had heard God speak and such individuals "did not lose social standing in the church through their failure to hear God speak."[61] The people she studied who had heard God speak to them were not compulsive about it and were very much involved in questioning if what they heard was "colored by their own psyche." "The experiences," she wrote, "were rare, brief, and startling but not distressing . . . the voices focused on immediate issues. They offered practical direction, not grand metaphysical theology."[62]

She also addressed the issue that claims to have heard God speak may be considered to be evidence of mental illness. Luhrmann notes that mentally ill individuals may believe God is speaking to them, but "the voice tortures,

---

[60] Ibid., xxiii.
[61] Ibid., 155.
[62] Ibid., 234.

it demands compulsive behavior. It does not question its validity.[63]

The experiences of the Christians Luhrmann studied did not display evidences of illness. They have developed a whole range of ways by which they attempt to discern the legitimacy of any such experiences. Luhrmann is not a member of the evangelical tradition in any sense and is not a convert. It was clear to her that these people were healthy, level-headed, and intelligent people who were well aware that they need to critically examine their experiences.

Luhrmann's conclusion was the same as that found by Daniel Smith and Elton Trueblood. Even though hearing the voice of God can be an expression of mental illness the evidence is clear that the healthy also can hear voices.

William James—the famous psychologist of a century ago—went further and included bizarre religious behavior when he contended that even the mentally ill in some cases could provide important religious insights. In his prestigious Gifford Lectures on *Natural Religion* in

---

[63] Ibid., 231-234.

1901-1902 he chose examples he admitted were "extremer" and acknowledged that these may have seemed to his hearers and readers to be "almost perverse" but he believed such examples gave "profounder information.[64] One example he included was that of George Fox, the founder of the Quakers. "Everyone who confronted [Fox] personally from Oliver Cromwell down to county magistrates and jailers, seemed to acknowledge his superior power. Yet from the point of view of his nervous constitution, Fox was a psychopath." James did not ignore his pathology but contended that even this did not necessarily negate his insights and contributions.[65] James recognized that to study reports of religious experience one would become acquainted with so many groveling and horrible superstitions that a presumption easily arises in his mind that any belief that is religious probably is false."[66] James, however, found even in bizarre religious experiences the individual can link experience to a larger consciousness and find meaning in this. He also called

---

[64] *The Varieties of Religious Experience* (New York: The Modern Library, 1999) 529. These lectures have remained in print over a hundred years and remain influential.
[65] Ibid., chapters 9—11.
[66] Ibid., 533.

for a "science of religion" that would compare reports of religious experience and believed this would provide useful insights.

James has been criticized for using bizarre religious experiences in his book in the belief that this has encouraged the stereotype that religious experience is pathological. Reports of bizarre human experience that claims an origin in religion can encourage the stereotype of religion as pathology. Such stereotypes can lead to the ignoring of the large body of writing to which Trueblood alluded. In fact, this has occurred. Trueblood was well aware of the seemingly wild, off beat, and varying claims to religious experience. His point was that all types of reports of religious experience should be studied.

There are several conventional interpretations that discount religious experience. One is that religious experience is a fantasy and that those who are psychologically needy may grasp it for that reason. It has been claimed that it is the insecure, gullible, suggestible and neurotic people who find comfort in religious experiences. All people have psychological needs and the needs vary but that does not mean that this is sufficient to explain all religious experience. Trueblood noted that the fact that there are "subjective conditions" does not mean that there is no "objective fact."[67] "The presence of one cause does not necessarily deny the presence of other and quite different causes."[68] Trueblood illustrates the notion of the single explanation, "We attribute a man's death to one factor, whereas the physician knows that death is usually attributable to a combination of factors. Germs cause death, if they are in the proper part of the body, if the person is in a receptive condition, etc. etc."[69]

Trueblood rejected the reductionist notion that religious experience is nothing but the human need to latch onto something because of insecurity. "It is not true," he wrote, "that the growing knowledge of God has uniformly given sweet comfort; it has driven men out into hardship and danger. . . . Man connects his religion in every generation, not with what he wants, but with his conception of what he ought to be and do."[70] Indeed,

---

[67] Trueblood, 166.
[68] Ibid., 170.
[69] Ibid., 169.
[70] Ibid., 182.

"prophets have normally protested against their cultural and political environment."[71]

A different approach that discounts religious experience as useful data is embedded in the sociological and anthropological traditions that regard God as a projection of culture. That is, a society constructs its idea of God in its own image. Durkheim and Malinowski, among others, thought they had confirmed this by comparative studies of a number of small cultures.

The evidence for this may seem convincing when we compare social and political views with religious views. If we compare views of race, gender, environmentalism, or economic systems; the record of society in recent decades reflects that beliefs for many Christians correlate with those of the society. As the culture has changed, the church has discovered new interpretations of the Bible that correspond with the new views in the society. For each of these examples—racial discrimination, gender roles, and environmentalism—the dominant positions of many churches have reflected the culture and these positions have evolved as has the culture.

---

[71] Ibid., 183.

There are, however, examples of the opposite. Phil Zuckerman examined and compared both the projection of American racial culture onto Christianity and the confrontation of American racial culture by Christian teachings.[72] Clearly, the support of slavery and later segregated discrimination by the churches reflected the racist culture but the movement to challenge segregation also was led by both black and white churches and their leaders. Religion can challenge the culture as well as be deeply influenced by it. Religion as a projection of culture is true but it is only part of the truth and, again, reducing it to one simplistic explanation distorts because it eliminates other major processes that are at work.

Religious experience is very likely to be influenced by the culture as well as psychological need but it also can alter both one's needs and one's understanding of the culture. Such factors do not invalidate the legitimacy of the experience itself. Religious experience does not support the reductionist contention that religious experience is "nothing but" a response to psychological need or

---

[72] *Invitation to the Sociology of Religion* (New York: Routledge, 2003) Chapter 5—6.

is culturally determined. As already noted, prophets normally protest against culture.

What can we conclude? Religious experience can be truly bizarre but it also can be quite ordinary. It can express pathology but it also can be quite healthy. What is clear is that people do have experiences that seem to be responses to God which may be through processes such as voices, visions, or dreams. But they also may have religious experience through writings or joining in activities with others. Humans have the capacity for such experience and the experiences are widespread.

The experience is real but does it originate from a God who talks? We return to the question of criteria. Phil Zuckerman quotes Carl Sagan approvingly that, "Extraordinary claims require extraordinary evidence." Zuckermann believes that the more unusual the claims "the more compelling (in both quality and quantity) must their evidence be."[73] He illustrates this in that if a claim is made that a dog ran by my house last night, this would be accepted without evidence. On the other hand,

---

[73] Ibid., 117—119.

if the claim is that thirty pink dogs ran by my house last night, one should be skeptical and demand more proof. Zuckerman does not identify what that proof might be for an event that happened last night. What I suspect he means is that such a story would be unlikely and he would reject it for that reason. With this illustration, he hopes to persuade us that religious experience is nothing more than psychological self-help disconnected from any objective reality.

Two observations come to mind. Religious experience is not a report of thirty pink dogs. It is the experience of millions of people around the world and over the centuries. It is a common experience though certainly far from universal. He is right to call for critical examination that is unbiased and inductive. He is mistaken to reduce religious experience to a simple psychological illusion.

The second thought is that empirical science balances the data available with the empirical methods possible. It is not functional to ipso facto demand a level of evidence and if this is not available refuse to consider the subject. Would it not be better to carefully assess what level of proof is achievable and then assess what level of confidence should be given to the idea? Scientists certainly vary in the level of confidence they have in one assessment as compared to another. The critical assessment is certainly in order but the a priori setting of level of proof required would seem to contribute nothing. It is an empirical question and without data we can only make projections based upon our own experience and the reports of others. That I consider something far-fetched does not mean that it is. To return to the prior point, to accept the quantum world as described by physics which no one has seen still seems far-fetched to me though I am confident there is good reason to accept it.

The experience of God is widespread. It is, however, ineffable just as are matters such as music, color, and love. All of these are real. What is ineffable can also be real though it needs to be examined in regard to its own nature. What is the evidence? What does it mean?

Polkinghorne has argued that there are no "knock down arguments" that inevitably compel us against our will to believe. Nevertheless, the existence of a widespread phenomenon does introduce one strand of evidence that should not be ignored. The experiences are real and possible meanings call for exploration. There is data to be considered, stereotypes to be unraveled, and judgments to be made about what is the best fit with what we know— that is, what is verisimilitudinous—and what it might mean. There are still more aspects to be considered.

Chapter

6

Linkage: An Ancient Covenant Kept

A separate empirical line of evidence is in the historical record. Judaism is an ancient faith with ancient traditions and ancient documents. Judaism also has claimed to have had an ancient covenant with an invisible God who was the creator and who would preserve them through this covenant. The purpose of this covenant, however, was not for the Jews alone but included a promise that it would be to the benefit of all people. (Gen. 18:18, 22:17—18). Judaism was called to be a "light to the nations" so that "salvation may reach to the ends of the earth." (Isa. 49:6) The historical record then is that the Jews are an ancient people with an ancient covenant that has survived and is very much still with us. Judaism is not just one religion among many. It has a unique history.

Science, as John Polkinghorne noted, cannot deal with unique events as its methodology requires control and replication. Nevertheless, methodological adjustment can be made here as in other applications of the scientific approach. While we understandably would like to have the pure science of the laboratory experiment, most science is not done this way because the nature of the data requires adjustment.

An accurate historical record is empirical. It is a record of empirical events. In some ways, Judaism is like other religions. It has codes of conduct. It has interpretation of the nature of God. While one can use the historical record to compare religions on selected variables, this ought not obscure the fact that Judaism is also unique. The historical record of its uniqueness can be studied. The claim that Judaism is unique and has a unique history is well documented. The fundamental question is: What does it mean?

The Jews were always a small clan and an insignificant

nation in terms of strategic and military power. There were innumerable such small groups in ancient times that have been lost from history having been absorbed into emerging larger nation states. Of the few names that have survived, there is no cultural continuity between their ancient times and their contemporary situation. A prime example is the ancient Philistines and the Palestinians of today. Their names are related and they have historically lived in the same area but they lack cultural connection. The identity of the vast majority of ancient peoples disappeared entirely.

Judaism was definitely one of those that we think should have disappeared. There were many situations where they were likely to disappear and be consolidated into other societies. Two of the many situations stand out as events that would seem guaranteed to be the end of Judaism in the world. The first was their destruction at the hands of the Babylonians in 586 BC. The second occurred when Rome leveled Jerusalem in AD 70. Neither proved to be the end. After the total destruction of Jerusalem by the Romans, the Jews had no homeland for 1,878 years—that is, from AD 70 to AD 1948—the Jews scattered and became a minority in many nations. As such they were persecuted repeatedly but they endured. The overwhelming scale of the holocaust is what comes to mind from recent history but there were many other times and places of extreme persecution.

Judaism, according to Max Dimont, is "one of history's most illogical survivals." He wrote that "it happened only once in history."[74] But they did survive. Paul Johnson characterizes the Jews as a dispersed people who "penetrated many societies and left their mark on all of them."[75] This has been true in spite of their being persecuted. When the United Nations created the state of Israel in 1948 they were once again in the place they had anciently claimed as the land God had promised them.

Israel remains today central in world affairs and a flashpoint of controversy even though the number of Jews today is a minuscule one-fifth of one percent of the world population. In terms of their numbers, the Jews are not important. In terms of contemporary world affairs, they are very important. They fulfill the promise to Abraham that his offspring would be a "light for the Gentiles [and]

---

[74] *Jews, God, and History* (New York: Signet Books, 1962), 13.
[75] *A History of the Jews* (New York: Harper and Row, 1988), 2.

that [God's] salvation would reach to the ends of the earth." (Isa. 49:6) The spiritual heirs of Judaism in Christianity and Islam do truly reach around the planet.

The Jews, Johnson points out, are the "only people in the world today who possess a historical record, however obscure in places, which allows them to trace their origins back into very remote times. [76] How far back can they be documented? Archaeologist Jodi Magness cites that the first known written reference to the people of Israel is the Merneptah stele in Egypt dated to 3,224 years ago.[77] Another archaeological finding being debated is a written mention that would have been recorded 3,425 years ago.[78] The Mesha Stele, dated at 840 BC, recorded how the King of Moab fought with Israel. The account parallels the Bible's account in 2 Kings 3:4—8. Various archaeological findings have confirmed places mentioned in the Bible but otherwise unknown.[79] We can be certain

---

[76] Paul Johnson, *A History of the Jews*, 7.

[77] Jodi Magness, *The Holy Land Revealed*, Chantilly, Virginia: The Teaching Company.

[78] "When Did Ancient Israel Begin?" *Biblical Archaeology Review*, 38:01, Jan-Feb. 2012.

[79] Paul Johnson, *A History of the Jews*, p. 5-15.

that the Hebrews—the earlier name for Israelites—are documented as a very ancient people.

To review the elements: An ancient people with ancient documents claimed to have a covenant with an invisible God. They claimed that this God was the only true God and unlike other gods this God was ethical and would keep the covenant that had been made. They claimed that though very small in number they would in time be a source of blessing to the whole world. They have been persecuted and there have been repeated attempts to destroy them but they continue. For almost two thousand years they did not even have a homeland. From their culture was born what became the largest religion—Christianity—and the second largest religion—Islam. These two religions are found around the world.

There is no other story like it. The pieces fit. Could it be evidence that the covenant with God was real as the Israelites have claimed all along?

Chapter

7

Linkage: Did the Creator Create Christianity?

*I*f the universe is the product of a Creator Mind, is there any reason to think that that Mind also created Christianity? Or, did Christianity just happen? Is there any empirical evidence that can link it to the Creator? What has happened in history can look inevitable in hindsight though it may not have been so at all. Because Christianity exists, it is easy to assume that its origin was not anything special. It just happened.

The unique covenant between God and the Jewish nation that is both ancient and historically supported includes, for Christians, the belief that Christ was the Jewish Messiah. This means that the Creator Mind that created the universe and formed the covenant with the

Jews was also the creator of Christianity through the revelation of God in the human life of Jesus.

There are available interpretations that are considered to explain the birth of Christianity as a natural process. This explanation would be along the lines that about two thousand years ago there was a charismatic teacher—Jesus—about whom there were claims that he performed miracles and promised eternal life to his followers. This persuaded people that he was the Son of God and a religion was created that within four hundred years became an accepted religion of the Roman Empire. It became the major religion of the world and was often allied with the political power of empires. There is nothing extraordinary about it. It is just what happened.

A closer look at this narrative is warranted and leads me to conclude that there was nothing inevitable about the establishment of Christianity. Consider briefly the explanation just given. First is the claim that it can be explained because Jesus was a charismatic teacher. This seems to be the case in that people did admire his teaching. It was claimed that, "No one ever spoke the way this man does." (John 7:46) Another comment was, "What's this wisdom that has been given to him?" (Mark 6:2) Crowds did seek him out but his reception was not always positive. Sometimes people heard him, left, and never returned. (John 6:66) Gifted teachers come and go and have great influence but it is for a relatively short time. Even ancients such as Homer and Plato who were remarkable and are still widely read are without particular impact. Some people find the writings of Homer and Plato interesting and quotable but their lives are not altered for having read them. Homer and Plato do not survive today having religious followers. There are very few charismatic teachers who have profound influence on peoples' lives that continue over centuries. That he was a charismatic teacher does not sufficiently explain the origins of Christianity.

In his teaching, Jesus did not promise power or wealth. Instead, he taught sacrifice, sharing, and giving. This has never been easy for people to accept and practice. It seems always to be a countercultural teaching. It is not something we find easy to accept. We still wrestle with this today: How much are we willing to share? This does not seem to be a successful strategy for starting a religion.

Secondly, in considering Jesus as one who worked miracles, Jesus acknowledged that some people had come and believed because of the miracles. (John 2:23; 4:48) However, those who saw his miracles were a relatively few people and only for a very limited time. After a few years, Jesus was gone and a generation arose that had not seen the miracles and knew no one who had. That someone somewhere worked miracles makes no impression when one has had no contact with them. It should also be noted that Jesus was not alone in working miracles as other people also claimed to have worked miracles. (Matt. 24:24; Mark 13:22) The spread of Christianity went far beyond the few people who would have been influenced by having seen the miracles.

Thirdly, concerning Jesus' teaching about heaven, promises of an after-life were already known. It was not a new or unique idea. There was a controversy at that time between the Pharisees who believed in an after-life and the Sadducees who did not. (Acts 23:6-8) That Jesus would side with the Pharisees on this one matter and speak of an after-life with a loving God would not have been unique and would not have propelled his listeners to form a new religion. The Pharisees did not attract such a following though they also taught that there was an after-life.

Finally, another explanation for the dominance of the Christian faith has been that over the centuries it has allied itself with political and military forces and these mutual alliances have been responsible for Christianity's spread. It is true that the church has formed alliances with powerful governments. This is a complex question but I will suggest some lines of thought.

There have been many times when the church has aligned with political powers and this has provided political support for the church and its spread. However, there are also ongoing events where Christians have stood in opposition to powerful governments. Alliances have helped spread the religion but they have also compromised it. In the Middle Ages for example, "monasteries became citadels of learning in a violent age—they were enclaves for Christians who in the name of Christ refused to take up arms."[80] The monasteries preserved the message of Christ

---

[80] Mark Kurlansky, *Nonviolence: Twenty-five Lessons from the History of a Dangerous Idea* (New York: Modern Library, 2006) 47.

against the war mongering of the Empire and its alliance with the church. Many groups such as the Mennonite Anabaptists have long challenged political powers. Yes, there have been alliances with political powers in the name of Christ and a result of such alliances has often been shameful and sinful accounts in the history of the church. Yet, the biblical roots have remained and have challenged the powers. Jesus' teaching is always a challenge to political power. Sometimes it is latent but it also has been assertive through the vicissitudes of human history.

Historical events can seem inevitable, as was earlier noted. They do not seem so when they are unfolding and it is inaccurate to regard them as such because we know the outcome. Historical records are always complex and I do not wish to oversimplify. It is helpful, however, to ask if all of the explanations for the reality of the Christian faith are adequate. Why is it that through generations of social and political flux and revolt, people rediscover and reconnect with this faith?

It is not accurate to see Christianity as just one of many religions. If we look for religions that have continued across geographical and cultural boundaries for extended periods of time there are only a few. Examples would be the Vedas, the Buddha, Mohammad, Moses and Jesus. Of these religions, the Vedas have crossed cultural borders in only a very limited way. Buddhism has recently held a considerable western influence but it is still limited. Islam has successfully crossed borders and cultures but it is an Abrahamic religion rooted in Judaism and Christianity. That is, it originated in the Judeo-Christian tradition.

This short list of religions is not to disparage the folk religions of isolated cultures. Neither is it to ignore the number of faiths derived from the world religions. Sikhism, for example, is an important religion that sought to integrate the Hindu and Islamic faiths. It is reasonable to examine each of these religions. There are commonalities among them in some ethical statements such as an opposition to murder. But there are significant differences as well. Christianity, then, is one of a very few world religions and it should be examined on the basis of its own record.

It is not easy to create a new religion that continues to exist for generations and that crosses cultural boundaries.

It is not sufficient to be a charismatic teacher with good and creative ideas. Christianity was launched and after twenty centuries it has spread around the globe. It is the faith far more people identify with than any other.[81] The truth of a religion, of course, cannot be measured by a head count. However, the examination of Christianity should not ignore its singular success over time and across cultures. It is found around the world.

Christianity is expressed in a wide range of denominations yet it has a solid core of ideas. That millions of people today identify themselves as Christians almost two thousand years after the writings in the New Testament, that they live thousands of miles from where these teachings were made and who consider these texts to be authoritative for living is remarkable. Furthermore, they read the texts as translated into many languages and find meaningful faith.

It seems to me to be well worthwhile to consider that it was uniquely remarkable that Christianity ever

---

[81] The counting of adherents to a world religion is extremely tenuous. There seems, however, to be a consensus among various assessments. One careful record is found in the often updated book, *Operation World*, by Jason Mandryk (Downers Grove IL: Intervarsity Press).

took hold. It was not at all inevitable. The founders of other world religions—such as Gautama, Moses, and Mohammad—died after having spent years developing their teachings, enlisting those who would carry on and organizing them. Jesus, however, died while still a young man who spent only three to four years recruiting and teaching his followers. This is a shorter period than it takes today to earn a college degree. Like students everywhere, Jesus' disciples often seemed very slow to pick up on his teaching. "How long shall I put up with you," was Jesus' comment when his disciples had failed to heal a man. (Matt.17:17) The disciples were clearly people with normal human flaws. They had spent such a brief time with Jesus but they dedicated their lives and spread his message. Christianity was born and thrived through their work without any organization or known plan for organizing.

Whatever one may claim about Christianity, it cannot be denied that something happened at the time Jesus lived. Albert Schweitzer wrote in the period around 1930 when many scholars were contending that there was no evidence that either Jesus or Paul had ever really lived. Schweitzer responded to these views in this way:

> It still has to be explained when, where, and how Christianity came into existence without either Jesus or Paul; how it came, later on, to wish to trace its origins back to these invented historical personalities; and finally for what reasons it took the remarkable course of making these two founders members of the Jewish people. The Gospels and the Epistles of St. Paul can, indeed, be demonstrated to be not genuine only when it is made intelligible how they could have come into existence if they really were not genuine.[82]

To review: The issue of the origins of Christianity is a complex historical question but there are some matters that we can know for certain. The creation of Christianity was an unlikely event. It has never been easy to create a new religion. That Jesus was a charismatic teacher, a worker of miracles, and one who promised heaven is not

---

[82] Albert Schweitzer, *Out of My Life and Thought* (New York: Henry Holt, 1933), 103.

sufficient to account for it. Alliances with political power have benefited but have also compromised the faith. The fact is that far more people today identify themselves with it than with any other religion. It is still not easy to embrace and practice the teachings of Jesus as we know if we take them seriously.

As already discussed, the creation of Christianity also fits into the narrative of the ancient covenant of the Jews. The promise to Abraham—as impossible as it seemed— is preserved in the contemporary Jewish communities and expanded around the world in Christian and Islamic traditions. It has gone around the world. It has, as promised to Abraham, blessed people in all nations.

In the debates about the meaning and validity of Christian claims, there are many factors to be weighed. What should not be forgotten is that something happened at that time and place which altered the course of the world. Schweitzer's observation is valid: the origins have to be explained. As imperfect as historical information can be, we can and should ponder that which we can know and this should not be negated by what we do not know. Whatever one concludes about the authenticity of the Christian faith, it is not simply "one of the religions." It has a unique origin and history. It occurred in conjunction with the ancient Jewish covenant. Something happened two thousand years ago that changed the world: What happened? Who was Jesus? What do we know? These fundamental questions and their answers are crucial.

Chapter

8

"To Whom Shall We Go?"

*A*t the beginning of this book there was a declaration of confidence in empiricism as the surest type of knowledge. Several types of empiricism have been utilized to suggest ways for the empirically minded individual to find grounding for the Christian faith. These are the inductive processes and the following is a review before we move to consider the deductive process.

The lesson from physics is that the material universe is not limited to what we can directly experience. There are sights that our eyes do not see and sounds that our ears do not hear because they fall outside the range of perception. The world would look and sound differently if the range of the eyes and ears were different. There is the quantum world quite different from anything we can know empirically. However, it is through making use of the unseen world that we have many applications including the cell phone. In using your cell phone you are using a world unseen in our everyday empirical experience. The suggestion was not to take the cell phone for granted but use it as a reminder of the unseen worlds. The claim of Christianity that there is an unseen God may or may not be true but the fact that it is unseen does not mean that it is not possible. Remember your cell phone.

If there is an unseen God, it is important to wonder what this God is like. It was noted that the empirical world we do experience can seem to be indifferent to human existence. Yet, meaningful human friendship is an important factor and the world does manifest the anthropic principle. That is, it is a world where all factors combine in a finely tuned balance that makes human life possible. This suggests for many that the world seems more likely to be the design of a mind than the proposed infinite number of universes with infinite chance processes to form the world we experience.

Turning to social science and human experience, it is a widespread human phenomenon that people have experiences that they regard as religious. There are many different types of experience involving a sense of presence from beyond the everyday life. These can involve hearing voices, seeing visions, having dreams, or a sense of presence. Some of these can be bizarre. Some can be triggered by mental illness. However, the phenomenon goes far beyond this and occurs widely among people of sound mind who think carefully and critically about the experience. Some of these experiences are personal and remain such. Some become integrated into religious traditions. Judaism, Christianity, and Islam all are basically collections of such experiences. As religious traditions are formed and evolve there will be many who join and participate who do not have such experiences but benefit from those whose experiences make up the tradition.

Historical data also contributes in the specific case of the Judeo-Christian tradition. Jews are a very ancient people with an early documented existence. They claimed to have a covenant with an invisible Creator God. In this covenant they were promised a continued existence and through them all of the peoples of the world would be blessed. That this small group survived with their identity is amazing. That from them came the two largest world religions—Christianity and Islam—is like no other account. The circumstances in the establishment of Christianity also portray a process that is not easy to explain. The other world religions had long-lived founders to solidify their ideas but Jesus died as a young man with only about three years devoted to teaching. The usual explanations for the successful implementation of Christianity do not bear careful examination. The advent and continuation of Christianity is also a unique story.

Each of these empirical references are complex matters to weigh. It is not easy to determine what conclusions are warranted. As Polkinghorne was earlier cited to say that, "There are no knockdown arguments" that one cannot help but believe. This is true of every view whether theistic or atheistic. All can lead to the question of verisimilitude: Looking at what can be known, what is the best fit for those matters that we cannot experience empirically? Can it be true that the reality that is claimed in Christianity is really true?

There was a situation in Jesus' life that has particularly fascinated me. A large crowd had gathered to hear Jesus speak. His message that day, however, was perplexing to them and they said it was a "hard saying"—a reaction we can understand today when we read the text. The crowd melted away. Jesus turned to the twelve apostles who remained and asked them, "You do not want to leave too, do you?" The extreme pathos for Jesus is evident. Then Peter spoke up, Lord, to whom shall we go, you have the words of eternal life?" The sermon puzzled the apostles as well. They did not, however, reassure Jesus that his teaching had really been a good lesson and Jesus did not blame the people who had left. Peter's statement volunteered only that even though they did not understand the teaching, they knew of no better alternative. What they affirmed was that they had found Jesus' teaching to be "life giving." (John 6:25—68)

When Peter referred to Jesus' teaching as being words of "eternal life" we may think that he is referring only to the promise of life after death. What Peter meant is unexplained in the context but the phrase he used refers to what is ageless having neither beginning nor end. Since human life has a beginning and an end and eternal life has only a beginning, the statement might be best understood that Peter and the other apostles followed Jesus because they believed he was revealing to them life-giving timeless truth. If this interpretation is correct, it does not negate Christian teaching about immortality. Rather, it is that on this occasion the disciples stayed with Jesus because they found him to be "life giving." Whatever the particular word meant, Peter was stating that they had found a better life in Jesus. He had found no attractive or compelling alternative.

Peter's statement is a useful, empirical standard—what ideas about life work best as life giving? There are many individuals who have given us meaningful sayings from which we can benefit. There are systems of thought that are beneficial. Sift them and reflect upon them. Evaluate the evidence. Ideas can be life giving without being revelation of Deity. That which is revelation, however, should be life giving.

The question of life giving quality becomes the deductive standard. We have considered empirical grounded factors that open up the possibility of a reality to the Christian claim. Being thus grounded, we now ask what the consequences are to practicing this faith. Does it give life?

The question is fair for all religions, anti-religions, and all philosophies we can find. For what it may be worth, I will briefly indicate my own conclusions. Agnosticism is appealing but it fails to help in the decisions that must be made. Atheism can appear to be simple, direct, and empirical. Yet it has its own problems as an affirmative claim. I find it helpful to read the publications of atheists for it helps me to clarify the problems atheism creates for itself.

For me, Jesus is "life giving" in the sense that if it were proven conclusively that Jesus were only a human teacher, I would still think that his teachings were "words of life" to be followed. Ranging from individual needs to the societal level, the words of Jesus compose a structure of ideas that can be found to be life giving—that is, to enrich life. They inspire and enrich personal experience. Even in those times when the sense of enrichment is missing, Peter's question is pertinent.

That Jesus appeals to me more than other teachers

may, of course, simply be the result of the fact that I was raised as a Christian. I cannot prove otherwise. I cannot "unraise" myself but I did for a period of time try to learn and read about other religions to see if I could find them also to be life giving. Reading the *Tao Te Ching*, I found that my favorite was Taoism. This, I came to realize, was at least in part a result of a sense that this was a spiritual practice which had some commonness with Christian spirituality. Buddhism was appealing in some of its perspectives. Hinduism and Shinto did not make any real sense to me. Islam and the Koran represented an offshoot from the Judeo-Christian tradition and did not seem to offer to me any additional contribution. And so I returned to Jesus for "words of life." This exploration was as fair as I could make it although in returning to my own upbringing I cannot prove that the decision was independent of that upbringing. As I have already noted, it seems to me to make sense that the Creator God might speak differently to different parts of the world. If God enlightened Buddha, so be it. For me, however, it has seemed that it is Christianity that is, as Peter declared, the "words of life."

If one is persuaded that Jesus has the words of life or wants to explore if this might be, there are factors to consider. Three are mentioned here. First, I have written as if Jesus' life and teaching is available. It is, but it comes with many different interpretations. What is the authentic Christian faith? There are churches and individuals whose practice of Christianity is not life giving but narrow, restrictive, and destructive. Indeed, it may be that this has been a part of life experience that has caused questioning or rejection. It is probably necessary to de-clutter one's mind of those ideas that seem destructive rather then life giving. The search must proceed to discover the best practices of the faith to try.

A second factor is that if we reject Jesus' words, on whose words will we find a better understanding? This should not be a casual thought but a serious examination. I return to the old aphorism mentioned earlier: "Whether or not we philosophize, we must philosophize." That is, we all live according to some set of ideas. What is crucial is to be aware of what ideas are guiding us and why we have accepted them as valid. It is not sufficient to reject Jesus and not examine what we have accepted. So Peter asked, "To whom shall we go?" We benefit by knowing to whom we have gone and to whom it is best for us to go at any point in life when this need strikes us and the search for a teacher is needed.

A third factor to consider is that Peter's question seems to assume a need to go to someone. Sometimes we may have this need but many people can live quite comfortably for periods of time without needing a teacher. As humans we have a self-awareness that compels us at times to seriously ponder the question, "Who am I?" Why do I have the unique capacity of awareness? Why do I ask why? Why do I know that I will die even when I am not in danger of death? Am I an animal with self-awareness? Or, am I a being—a spirit is one useful term—that has a body? There are so many questions. We can avoid them and just live, but they are still there and at times they intrude in our consciousness. Undeniably we have a body and that body has had and does have a crucial impact upon who we are but it is not the most important part of being. The most important is the being—that is, the spirit—that each of us is.

However you respond to these considerations—at this moment they may seem laborious—the "you" that you are is a person whose spirit has been shaped by a particular time and place. It is the particular family, the particular school, the particular books you have read. It reflects the particular successes and failures you have experienced. It reflects the particular ideas you have incorporated into your thought processes. These are the sources for how we live. At some particular points in every life, experience moves beyond what one has previously found to be satisfactory. The cultural background of one's identity that in the past seemed at least relatively settled then poses unsettling questions. A new teacher or a new understanding of the previous teacher is then needed either to develop new understandings or to reinterpret the previous ones. Where then do you find this teacher? Peter's understanding had greatly expanded under the teaching and companionship with Jesus. Confused by Jesus' teaching and asked by Jesus if he also was going to leave, Peter declared both that he needed a teacher and that he knew of no better alternative. Neither do I.

Each of the empirical, grounded topics that have been introduced can put one on an extensive and productive search. They can open for us the understanding that there are empirical reasons to suspect that Jesus might be a revelation from God. The deductive test can then be made with confidence that we are not considering a placebo faith. Searching for the authentic expressions of Christ leads to the deductive questions: Who was Jesus? Are his teachings words of life?

Printed in the United States
By Bookmasters